MORE PRAISE FOR <u>Z.B.A.</u>

"Marc does a brilliant job blending the spiritual and the practical in a likeable style of simplicity, genuineness, and self-deprecating humor. His book shows us how the philosophies and practices of Zen will give us resilience in the face of challenges; win the hearts and minds of employees, customers, and business partners; and deliver a unique kind of competitive edge in the world of business."

— **Minh Le, president of The Wilfred Jarvis Institute**

"In a world of intense competition and drive for short-term profits, Marc Lesser brings a new and vital message. The world of work is not about profits, promotions, bonuses, and self-interested behavior. True work is the art of living life — a life of vitality, of completeness, of interdependence with our fellow workers, our environment, our loved ones, and most important, with ourselves."

— **John Oliver Wilson, retired executive vice president and chief economist of Bank of America**

"I have long realized that among spiritual paths, Zen is uniquely suited to application in the world of work. The way is right there at your fingertips, not complicated, but it does require a guide, someone who knows Zen practice — and the ins and outs of real-world business. In *Z.B.A.* Marc Lesser has managed with elegant and honest lucidity to point to a Zen way of working. This book isn't Zen in ten easy steps; it's a reliable companion for the path."

— **Norman Fischer, former abbot of the San Francisco Zen Center and author of *Taking Our Places***

"*Z.B.A.* is a wake-up call for any entrepreneur who seeks self-knowledge, life balance, and boundless vitality. You'll save yourself years of practice just by contemplating the provocative questions at the end of every chapter."

— **Will Rosenzweig, former president and CEO of The Republic of Tea**

Z.B.A.

ZEN OF BUSINESS
ADMINISTRATION

Z.B.A.

ZEN OF BUSINESS ADMINISTRATION

HOW ZEN PRACTICE CAN TRANSFORM YOUR WORK AND YOUR LIFE

MARC LESSER

NEW WORLD LIBRARY
NOVATO, CALIFORNIA

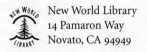 New World Library
14 Pamaron Way
Novato, CA 94949

Interior design and typography by Tona Pearce Myers

Lines from the poem "A Book for the Hours of Prayer" by Rainer Maria Rilke on page ix quoted from *Selected Poems of Rainer Maria Rilke*, edited and translated by Robert Bly, copyright © 1981 by Robert Bly. Reprinted with permission of Harper Collins Publishers Inc.

Library of Congress Cataloging-in-Publication Data
Lesser, Marc, 1952–
  Z.B.A., Zen of business administration : how Zen practice can transform your work and your life / by Marc Lesser.
      p.   cm.
Includes index.
ISBN 1-57731-469-7 (pbk. : alk. paper)
1. Management—Religious aspects—Zen Buddhism. 2. Work—Religious aspects—Buddhism. 3. Religious life—Zen Buddhism. I. Title: ZBA, Zen of business administration. II. Title.
HD31.L3844 2005
650.1—dc22   2004021300

First printing, February 2005
ISBN 1-57731-469-7

 Printed in Canada on 100% postconsumer waste recycled paper

g A proud member of the Green Press Initiative

Distributed to the trade by Publishers Group West

10   9   8   7   6   5   4   3   2   1

To my parents, Ralph and Beatrice Lesser,
who never quite understood the
choices I made and yet were always supportive and trusting.

I live my life in growing orbits
which move out over the things of the world.
Perhaps I can never achieve the last,
but that will be my attempt.

I am circling around God, around the ancient tower,
and I have been circling for a thousand years,
and I still don't know if I am a falcon, or a storm,
or a great song.

— Rainer Maria Rilke

CONTENTS

WISDOM: YOUR ORDINARY MIND IS THE PATH

LISTENING TO YOUR CLEAR, QUIET VOICE

YOU CAN CHANGE THE WORLD

INTRODUCTION

"Don't be a board-carrying fellow." This expression, sometimes used in Zen, refers to a carpenter carrying a long, wide wooden board on his shoulder, blocking his view in one direction. It is an admonition about seeing the world and ourselves as ordinary and mundane without also considering the sacred, mysterious, and unfathomable aspect of our hearts, minds, and surroundings.

This expression can also help us understand that our work is not separate from our lives. One side, an important and vital side of work, involves goals, achievements, money, ambition, and developing your career. Understanding and implementing the technical and strategic aspects of your work are critical for your organization or business to fulfill its mission.

What about the other side? We are all human beings. We all bring a vast set of rich and complex experiences, skills, patterns, needs, aspirations, and emotions to our work. The other side, often more difficult to see, is the sacred aspect of your work, the way in which your work can expose and transform habits and patterns in your life while uncovering your authentic, compassionate, inner wisdom.

When you remove the board from your shoulder, a new world opens, a new way of understanding yourself, of seeing others and the true meaning of your work. Removing the board doesn't mean turning your work into a self-help workshop. As a business owner with an M.B.A., I understand the importance of results, hiring and motivating talented people, sales and marketing, strategic planning, and cash flow management, as well as the many skills required to start, manage, and grow a business. As a human being and a Zen priest, I also understand we all bring our full selves to work: our wishes, dreams, desires, anger, and frustration, as well as a deep yearning to find real inner peace, freedom, and happiness.

In these pages I offer many of my experiences, my mistakes, the lessons I've learned, things to try, ways I have laughed at myself and sometimes cried, and many, many questions. I feel honored and humbled to present my experiences and to offer some basic and not-so-basic practices. Honored, because I am passionate about the importance of integrating business practice and spiritual practice, the delight I feel in sharing my journey, and the potential I see for conscious, awakened businesspeople to transform our world. Humbled, because the skills and abilities required to run successful organizations and businesses, even while they open our hearts to being fully authentic human beings, are immensely challenging.

One of the most famous pieces in Zen literature, read or chanted every day in Zen practice centers, is called the Heart Sutra, which in a few paragraphs describes the essential path of Zen practice. A phrase from the Heart Sutra says, "without any hindrances, no fears exist." These hindrances are the ways in which we protect ourselves, shield our hearts, and keep ourselves closed and separate. Zen practice provides a method·and discipline for identifying and loosening the ways we get in our own way. It helps us move from living and acting from fear, to living and acting with fearlessness. By searching for safety and control, and from responding out of fear, without realizing it, we sacrifice the freedom, flexibility, and connections that are our birthright.

Business practice could also be described as the method and discipline of removing hindrances. The challenge of business is to identify and remove what gets in the way of manifesting and implementing a wide and creative vision, to remove the obstacles to distributing people and resources where they are needed, and to remove the obstacles to actually meeting the needs of all people in our communities and on our planet. What would a world without hindrances, without fear, look like?

Though this task of integrating our full selves with our work may at times appear daunting, the challenge and the effort are not separate from the path. This book provides tools, ideas, and insights that may give you the courage and confidence to make the effort to see yourself, your work, and the world as they truly are. Integrating Zen practice and business practice allows us to find our work and ourselves, beyond our ideas, and to experience both the ordinariness and the immensity of our lives.

Z.B.A.

ZEN OF BUSINESS
ADMINISTRATION

WE ARE ALL ZEN STUDENTS,
WE ARE ALL BUSINESSPEOPLE

WE ARE ALL ZEN STUDENTS,
WE ARE ALL BUSINESSPEOPLE

In the fall of 1983 I left Tassajara, Zen Mountain Center, with my wife and infant son, and went to New York City to attend my last semester of Rutgers University in New Jersey to complete my undergraduate degree and to enter New York University's Graduate School of Business. At Tassajara I had been a Zen monk and a respected administrative leader. In New York City I was a thirty-one-year-old unemployed new father, without a college degree and with no experience that anyone could relate to. My résumé showed that I had been director of Tassajara and had spent the last ten years living at the San Francisco Zen Center and the last four years as a Zen monk.

Shortly after arriving in New York I went into Manhattan to an employment agency to find temporary work. I put on my best (and probably my only) suit and tie and arrived on the fifty-second floor of a skyscraper on Madison Avenue in the office of an agency that someone suggested I visit. I gave my résumé to the receptionist and sat in the waiting area. After a few minutes I looked up and saw several people gathered around a desk looking at my résumé, smiling, laughing, and looking at me. I overheard someone say in amazement, "There's a Zen monk in our office looking for a job!" As you might imagine, I had a hard time finding work in New York City.

Despite my difficulties finding a job, a basic truth that I have come to learn, and a primary assumption of this book, is that we are all Zen students, and we are all businesspeople. We are all Zen students in that we all must contend with birth, old age, sickness, and death. We have no idea where we come from or where we will go. At the deepest level we all have the same aspirations — to love and be loved, to discover and express our unique gifts, and to find peace and equanimity in the midst of whatever life may bring us. Zen is a practice and set of values to help us be aware, to awaken, to uncover our innate wisdom and authenticity. Though Zen is often perceived as enigmatic and difficult to understand, it is at its heart a system of simple practices that can be done anywhere — even in the middle of our busy work lives.

We all have to deal with difficulty and crisis — taking care of dying parents, troubled friends, or children; meeting the changes that come suddenly or gradually; confronting pain and difficulty for ourselves and for those we love. Meditation practice and Zen practice are much like creating a controlled crisis — we have nowhere to go and nothing to do; we're depending on our own bodies and minds, completely alone, and completely connected. Zen practice can help us reveal ourselves, our pain and suffering, our bare feelings, the immensity of our lives. By sitting still, just by being present, we learn that we can fully accept our imperfect selves, just as we are. This process can be cleansing and transforming; it can influence every part of our lives. Zen practice is ultimately about finding real freedom and helping others.

And we are all businesspeople. There is no avoiding having to deal with money, with the basic needs we all have for food and shelter and clothing. All professions, even those not primarily focused on business, are embedded in the world of business. Doctors and

therapists call their customers patients. Teachers and social workers cannot escape budgets and management structures. Nonprofit
organizations and religious institutions need to attract employees,
pay salaries, and perform within financial frameworks.

At the heart of all businesses, whether they are overtly within
the business community or not, is a focus on meeting the needs of
people. Businesses make things or provide services that people
need. We sometimes forget that the starting point of business is
much more than making money or creating wealth. During the
recent bursting of the dot-com bubble we learned firsthand what
happens when businesses are started without a thoughtful plan for
meeting the needs of people: they often disappear rather quickly.

In 1973 I took a one-year leave of absence from Rutgers, where
I had been majoring in psychology. A year later, when I first
entered the San Francisco Zen Center building, I heard a clear,
quiet voice saying that this place, this practice, was worth ten years
of my life. I was drawn to the discipline of a daily meditation practice and the blending of a deep, mystical philosophy with a
grounded, practical approach. I was impressed by the maturity,
sincerity, and wisdom of the teachers and students. I was intrigued
by the possibility of living within a community of like-minded
people and by the concept of work as an expression of spiritual
practice.

During my tenth year at the San Francisco Zen Center I was
asked to be director of Tassajara, Zen Mountain Center, a monastery
in a mountainous wilderness area in central California. I loved my
work as director and was surprised when I first noticed that though
I was living the life of a Zen monk, my daily work activities were primarily business related — managing people, overseeing budgets,
solving problems, and devising strategic plans. I came to realize not

only that there was no conflict between spiritual practice and business practice but also that these two activities were vital complements to each other. I was a more effective manager because of my Zen practice; and my Zen practice was more focused and vibrant through the disciplines and challenges of my management activities.

While at Tassajara I began thinking about what would come next for me, feeling it was time to move outside the sphere of the Zen Center community. Again I began to hear a clear and quiet voice saying that it was time to enter the business world. I thought for sure that this voice must be mistaken or that it was whispering to the wrong person. And yet, in some peculiar way, it made perfect sense.

I aspired to combine my Zen training and my intention to make a difference in the world with the belief that it might be possible to integrate spiritual practice and business practice within the business community. I reasoned that since this was what I was doing at the Zen Center, there must be some way to take this activity to the business world. I also observed that business now played a prominent and influential role in our world. After many years of training in spiritual practice, I felt that I needed some business training, so I decided to get an MBA.

This was the opening paragraph of my business school application, written while I was director of Tassajara, after having been a resident of the San Francisco Zen Center for ten years:

I have always been a "manager." At age six I was organizing the children on my block to protect themselves from the bully on the next block. In Little League baseball I led the Suburban Delicatessen team to win the "world series." In high school I was the captain of the varsity wrestling team, and in college was vice president of Theta Chi fraternity. In 1978 I spent two months with my father as he was dying of cancer — managing his care by directing doctors, nurses, and family members and making intimate contact with him by stepping outside established medical and family systems. At Zen Center, Green Gulch Farm, I implemented the revival of the nineteenth-century practice of draft horse farming and demonstrated its potential for being cost effective. At Tassajara, Zen Mountain Center, I was the assistant cook and then the head cook, the head of the meditation hall, and the director of Tassajara. Managing, therefore, has been a vehicle for self-development for most of my life.

Journeying to New York City, to business school, to life outside the Zen Center community, as a husband and new father, was a painful, challenging, and tremendously rich time. In many ways I felt like a visitor from another planet. I had left my community, which had become my family, my place, and in many ways my identity. Yes, this is ironic, since Zen practice is aimed at helping us not become too attached to things, particularly one's identity. It was a rude awakening to see that I had become quite comfortable with being a Zen student. Looking back, this was one of the most important transitions in my life.

I spent two years as a full-time student at New York University's Graduate School of Business located just off Wall Street in Lower Manhattan. My second job out of business school was as a manager for Conservatree Paper Company in San Francisco, where I was responsible for purchasing and selling large quantities of recycled paper. I learned the basic skills involved in commerce, or what I've come to think of as trade skills. One of my customers was a small mail-order business that offered greeting cards and wrapping paper made from recycled paper. I watched this company expand from being a two-person operation to becoming a major catalog company. They were the only company in the United States making paper goods from recycled paper. Yet I didn't find their designs particularly attractive. I suggested to the owner of Conservatree that we diversify into the catalog business, but this idea was met with little interest. So I began writing a business plan. I had become knowledgeable in the field of recycled paper, I had many friends from Zen Center who were artists, and I saw a market that was in its infancy and growing quickly. Thus the idea for Brush Dance was born.

Brush Dance began in my garage in 1989. We started as a mail-order catalog producing a few wrapping papers and greeting cards made from recycled paper. Today we are a multimillion dollar company that sells cards, journals, calendars, and gift items to stores throughout the United States and the world. The company's byline is Mindful Stationery Products, The Art of Meaningful Expression. Brush Dance products can be found at more than five thousand retail outlets. Our customers include Borders, Barnes & Noble, Bed, Bath and Beyond, and Target, as well as small stores selling cards, gifts, and books. Our licenses include Renee Locks, His Holiness the Dalai Lama, Thich Nhat Hanh, and the Poetry of Rumi.

During my years of growing a business I have continued my daily meditation practice as well as maintained a strong connection with the San Francisco Zen Center. Last fall I traveled to Japan to attend the thirty-third memorial service of Suzuki Roshi, the founding teacher of the San Francisco Zen Center and author of *Zen Mind, Beginner's Mind.* I stayed for several days before the ceremony with Suzuki Roshi's son, Hoitsu (referred to as Hojo-san), who has become one of the leading Zen teachers in Japan today. Being with Hojo-san, his wife, and family in this five-hundred-year-old temple was life changing. Hojo-san loved to laugh and play and was extremely attentive. We sat together on the floor each evening for dinner. Whenever I took a sip of sake, Hojo-san was quick to refill my cup.

As I was leaving the temple, Hojo-san gave me a drawing that he had made of a frog and a Zen monk sitting in meditation, with the frog looking at the monk and the monk looking at the frog. He had written some beautiful Japanese characters above the figures. When I asked Hojo-san what the characters meant, he said, "Everywhere you go is your temple." These simple and profound words have stayed with me and became the foundation for this book and for my life.

I have been managing and growing Brush Dance for fifteen years. I feel fortunate to be running a company with a mission to disseminate spiritual messages to the world. The financial, operational, and personnel challenges continue to provide never-ending practical and spiritual challenges. At the same time Zen practice has become more and more a central focus in my life: I've been lecturing and teaching at the San Francisco Zen Center, I co-lead retreats for businesspeople at Zen Center's Green Gulch Farm, and I was recently ordained as a Zen priest.

We are all Zen students, and we are all businesspeople. Our lives are messy, impossible, miraculous, mysterious, and beyond our usual explanations. There are no easy answers. It can be difficult to learn to appreciate the questions. What does it mean to be fully ourselves at work? How can we find true fulfillment and happiness? How can we find true fulfillment and happiness at our jobs? What is the impossible request our life makes of us? What outer or inner transformations are required before we can see our work life as a place to practice, as a sacred space? What does "Everywhere you go is your temple" really mean?

The temple referred to by Hojo-san may be very different from any notion we have about what a temple is supposed to look like. This temple might sometimes appear to be a bedroom, a mountain trail, a factory assembly line, or an office filled with desks and computers. It is a very large, inconceivably wide temple. I feel fortunate to be asking these questions and walking a path with so many sincere people. We are all Zen students, and we are all businesspeople, and we are all so much more.

START WHERE YOU ARE

When I first had the idea of starting a business, I couldn't think of anything else. It was difficult to sleep, sometimes to eat. I could physically feel something inside me aching to come out, aching to be born. My thoughts and dreams were filled with this urge, still unformed. It was the nearest I have come to the experience of being "pregnant." My life was turned upside down.

The first time I shared what I felt growing inside me it felt like I was taking a huge risk. What if this was just some crazy idea — the idea of starting a business of making greeting cards and wrapping papers from recycled paper? What if I was just fooling myself and this was just a dream? I said it out loud, and the idea began to take root and grow. The aching intensified.

I needed some help, some outside, seasoned perspective. I decided to contact Rudy, a successful businessman I first met while I was director of Tassajara. He had a reputation for having impeccable integrity. He was trained as an engineer, and one of his first businesses was formed when he invented a labeling machine — this machine became the Dymo labeler. Since growing and selling this company Rudy had begun and sold many companies. Rudy was now "retired" — consulting for a host of start-ups.

On a foggy summer day I drove across the Richmond Bridge

on my way to Rudy's office in Berkeley. I was nervous and excited. Having lived in a Zen monastery for many years, I was familiar with the feeling I always had when I was going to see my Zen teacher, who in this case happened to be a businessman. Rudy asked lots of pointed questions regarding the market, the strategic advantages, competition, price points, margins, and capital needed for start-up. He liked the basic idea that I described but suggested I write a comprehensive business plan in which I address the issues he raised. I left feeling both excited and discouraged. I was impatient to get started. Now I had more work to do.

Three weeks later I came back to meet with Rudy with my first real business plan. He felt that I had made progress, and he had many more questions and concerns regarding marketing strategies, inventory management, and operations. He questioned whether the gross margins of recycled paper were high enough to support the business overhead. We agreed that there was more to research and understand. Again I left feeling that I was making real progress, and I was even more discouraged and impatient.

Three weeks later I returned with a revised and more fully developed plan. I felt much like a Zen student wanting to be admitted to the monastery — knocking at the door and being told to go away, each time the teacher sending the student away as a means of testing his resolve. I looked at Rudy as he silently read my plan. His face seemed serious and concerned. He looked up at me and said, "Well, I think you are ready." Within a few weeks I borrowed a total of $30,000 from my mother, my brother, from Rudy, and from several friends and began producing greeting cards and wrapping papers made from recycled paper, as well as a one-page brochure. I had started a business. I was elated and terrified. It took several months for the name Brush Dance to appear.

Integrating Zen practice with your work requires all of you — your complete attention, effort, and commitment. Even speaking about integrating Zen and work misses the mark and can create confusion. There is no such thing as Zen practice outside of who we are and what we do. There is no such thing as work separate from your life. Work is not something you do to earn money or make a living. Everything you do is your life, your path. Your work is your path. Relationships are your path. Uncovering your innate clarity and wisdom is your path, wherever you go and whatever you do. This is a subtle yet powerful reframing of our lives.

The word I use to describe this integration is *practice,* as in practicing the piano or a legal practice or baseball practice. In our lives, everything is practice, and at the same time everything is performance. As my high school wrestling coach used to say, you perform just like you practice; there's no difference. Reframing your life and seeing that all your actions are practice requires us to undergo a subtle and complete transformation.

We each have no choice but to start where we are with what we have. This is our challenge, our life, our practice. Each obstacle, problem, handicap is part of the practice. Every advantage, every success helps to clarify and define our practice.

Entering this path and reframing our work and our lives as practice come with a variety of requirements:

- a way-seeking mind

- regular practice

- retreat time

- a relationship with a teacher or mentor

- support from a group
- a commitment to study and practice

Let's explore each of these.

A WAY-SEEKING MIND

You may experience being alive as a miracle; you may feel that life is often difficult and at times impossible. You deeply understand how short our lives are and that we are each on this planet for an extremely limited time. These experiences often come through feeling pain. The pain may be from ending a relationship, from losing a job or a business, from the death of a loved one, or from any difficult change in your life. Pain is often the stimulus that can open our hearts and minds. Our pain opens us to see our fundamental connection with all other human beings on the planet.

At the same time you deeply understand the possibility for change, the potential for finding real freedom by acknowledging and loosening habitual thinking and actions. You come to understand that the solution is not more money, fame, control, or power. You acknowledge that the only way to find real peace and happiness, for yourself and for others, is coming to a deeper understanding of yourself. You realize that the seeds to your own happiness and freedom lie within you. You know that you and the world are vast and mysterious, and you are determined to penetrate the issues of life and death, suffering and happiness.

Possessing a way-seeking mind is the same as having the insight that freedom and happiness are possible and that much effort is required. You come to understand that your work is your life and that your life is your work. You see that work is an opportunity to go deeper, to find satisfaction, to awaken to your true nature.

It is difficult for me to pinpoint what first brought me to practice, my original experience of the way-seeking mind. Was it my childhood vow to help my father through his mental illness, the pain of my first girlfriend leaving me and exposing my vulnerability, or seeing the television show *Kung Fu* (about a young boy receiving spiritual instruction from a Buddhist priest) and thinking, "that's how I want to live my life"? Or perhaps it was reading Alan Watts's book *The Way of Zen* when I was a freshman in college and realizing that nothing else seemed more important than freeing myself from habitual thinking so that I could help others.

REGULAR PRACTICE

Zen is more than a philosophy, more than a way of thinking. Zen is a practice. It is something that you *do,* preferably every day. You cannot think your way into being present, into altering habits and patterns formed over a lifetime. You cannot simply read books. Zen requires a regular meditation practice — a time to pay attention to your mind and body. It requires taking what you learn from your way-seeking mind into your work, relationships, and everyday life. It requires your life to be guided by values of openness, honesty, and compassion.

I sit meditation nearly every morning, usually by myself, for twenty or thirty minutes. I chant, put on my robes, and do three full bows. One morning and evening a week I sit with a small group. When I arrive at work, I take a few moments to acknowledge my intention to practice at work. I often light some incense and take a few moments of quiet time as a way of setting my intention. Above my desk hangs the painting given to me by Hojo-san in Japan. You will remember that the calligraphy next to these figures says, "Everywhere you go is your temple." I also attend a weekly seminar in which a small group studies Zen-related texts.

RETREAT TIME

We all need time outside the routines and stresses of our busy lives. There is tremendous wisdom in observing the Sabbath, setting aside one day a week as a retreat, a time devoted to just being and not doing. If you can't set aside one day a week, then perhaps schedule one day a month. Some can manage only a three-day or five-day retreat once a year. That's okay too. However you manage it, just having some time to stop, to reflect, and to rejuvenate yourself is an essential practice.

Each month I do a one-day retreat with small group in the Marin Headlands. I spend the day sitting, walking, and conversing with good friends. Sometimes I meet with a teacher as part of the retreat. At least once a year I try to do an extended retreat, usually seven days long. And, as I mentioned above, I generally take fifteen to twenty minutes every day at work to sit or walk quietly by myself.

A RELATIONSHIP WITH A
TEACHER OR MENTOR

Putting Zen practice into your work life requires the guidance of a person you trust. Everyone needs the guidance and support of an experienced teacher or mentor. This person might come in the form of a good friend, another practitioner, a therapist, or a religious figure. We all need models, and we all need others we can go to for support and guidance.

I have a variety of teachers and mentors, from the Zen world and from the business world. Most of these relationships are quite informal. When I need help or advice, I arrange a meeting or a phone call. I also act as a teacher and a mentor for several others. Since so many people have been generous and available to me, I make my best effort to be available to those wanting help, advice, or an ongoing relationship.

SUPPORT FROM A GROUP

We all need others to help us see ourselves and our patterns more clearly. An important element of developing yourself and changing your habits is to meet with a group that supports your commitment to develop your practice. This can be a group of friends, of others on a similar path, or people from the business community working to integrate their values into their work.

Because I am fortunate to live in a part of the world where Zen groups and spiritual groups are readily accessible, I take part in several groups. I generally spend one night a week at the San Francisco Zen Center. Several times a year I give talks at the Zen Center and lead workshops at Green Gulch Farm. In traveling around the country I'm often surprised to find sitting groups or spiritual groups in almost every city or town.

A COMMITMENT TO STUDY AND PRACTICE

Integrating Zen practice into your work and your life cannot be done in a weekend or semester course. It is an ongoing process, without beginning and without end. It requires study and practice, resolve and diligent effort. As Jack Kornfield, a leading meditation teacher, puts it in the title of one of his books, "After the ecstasy, the laundry."

For many people, the decision and commitment to begin practicing is a major step. This commitment might be to sit meditation once a month, to meet with a group of friends once a week, or to sit for ten minutes at the beginning of each day. One of my most valuable support groups meets one weekend a year. This is a group of eight men who had previously lived and practiced together at the San Francisco Zen Center and are now all living and working in the "world." For one weekend each year we sit, tell our stories, listen to each other, laugh, cry, and play. At the end of the weekend we put it on our calendars to meet the following year.

One of my reasons for becoming ordained as a Zen priest was to make my commitment to Zen practice public. Being ordained is also a statement that my effort and focus are to help others with their practice.

SERENITY IS NOT FREEDOM FROM THE STORM BUT PEACE WITHIN THE STORM

When my daughter was ten I read to her in bed every night before she went to sleep. Often I would begin to fall asleep before she did, and she would gently tap my face to wake me up. One night, after I had finished reading and was tucking her in, she looked at me and asked, "Daddy, when we die, do we find out all the answers, all the secrets to life? You know, like in a game or puzzle, when you are finished you can look at the back and find out all the answers." I must confess that though I remember the question clearly, I'm not sure how I responded. I hope I said something like, "I think that the answers are within us all the time and are regularly being revealed to us, if we just pay attention. We don't need to wait until we die to discover our truth."

People often think of Zen as a way to feel less or to be less emotional. Yet in reality Zen practice tends to make us *more* aware of our emotions. An expression I like is "Serenity is not freedom from the storm but peace within the storm." Getting closer to our truth may lead us to feeling more joy and at the same time more pain; we may feel more at home at work or more estranged, depending on the truth of our situation. While becoming more calm and centered and perhaps detached from any outcomes, you may find that your emotions and your compassion become more fully developed.

Zen, like our lives, is filled with paradox. On the one hand, some things just seem to happen beyond our control; a seemingly insignificant event can change our lives. On the other, most change requires intention, focus, and discipline. I generally subscribe to the theory that through lots of hard work and sweat we become more open to the "insignificant" events that can change our lives.

Another paradox is that at the heart of Zen practice is what Suzuki Roshi calls "no gaining idea." Most inspirational writing, how-to books, and books on personal growth aim to take you from point A to point B; they often convey the idea that the process of improving ourselves consists of a beginning, a middle, and an end. They tell us that if we just think of things in a different way we will be happier or more enlightened. In contrast, Zen aims at pointing out what we already know, opening the way toward seeing who we are and what is already around us. It is more about peeling away what we have added on than it is about adding on new things.

Another Zen expression is "A father who thinks he is a good father is not a good father." This saying guides us to appreciate our moment-by-moment efforts and intentions and to move away from the habits of judgment, achievement, and results. Being a good father, being "good" at anything is more about the process, the effort, the giving of ourselves, of our attention and our vulnerability, than it is about achieving a result that we can point to or measure. If we think we have arrived at our goal and can now shrink our efforts, think again! The stories and practices in this book are reminders that while we are in the midst of our busy lives, we always have opportunities to be ourselves, to be truthful, to act from our hearts.

Herein lies another paradox. And perhaps this is where business practice has something to offer Zen practice: results do matter, success and failure are real, accountability and measurement are important. These truths are vital to business and cannot be avoided. Results are also essential to spiritual growth, although they can be more difficult to quantify. The problem is that in a narrowly defined business practice, the tendency is to measure results solely in financial terms and not in how the business is meeting people's needs. It is this kind of one-sided thinking that allows businesses to pollute the environment and destroy natural re-sources and that can cause discrimination and violence, as well as a sense of defeat in people's hearts, homes, and throughout the world.

Zen practice emphasizes the need for both sides: the world of form, the world of our senses and our perceptions, and the world that is beyond either the spiritual or the material, often referred to mysteriously as "emptiness." There is another famous Zen expression, "Form is emptiness and emptiness is form." Form is the world of things, of results. We all want safety and control and predictability. This is natural for all human beings everywhere. Emptiness is the world of our intuition, of our connection, of what we intuitively know but cannot explain. It is the realization that we have no idea how we were born into this world, that the moment we are born we begin to die, and that the world is mysterious and sacred beyond our wildest imaginations. It is in balancing emptiness and form that businesspeople and businesses can act responsibly. Imagine if all business decisions included both the world of form and the world of emptiness.

These practices do come with risks. Sometimes really looking at the truth of our situations and seeing how much of us we leave out of our business lives can be very painful. At a recent retreat for businesspeople that I was co-leading, we discovered that several people who had taken the workshop in the past had returned — and most of them had left their jobs! Not doing these practices also comes with risks — especially the risk of not being our full selves, not doing what we really want to do, using the excuse that we are just "at work."

We are all faced with the constant tension between how we care for people and how we manage the challenges that confront us, between maintaining control and letting go, between aiming for perfection and accepting things the way they are. We all bring our unique patterns and habits to our management styles — our deepest wounds and greatest strengths, our level of security and self-esteem, our skills and experiences, our mentors and models for what makes a good manager.

For many years I was the primary "manager" of the early-morning routines in my house — waking my children, making breakfast and lunches, getting the kids to the kitchen table and to school on time. Every day the challenges were unique — some days there were no clean socks, or someone overslept, or one or both kids just didn't feel like eating. Once we sat down to breakfast, we often experienced a few moments of calm. At other times I would have to remind my kids that breakfast is a noncontact sport! After dropping them off at their schools, I felt a sense of relief and accomplishment. The rest of the day, being CEO of a small, growing, complex company often seemed easy in comparison to the task of getting my children to school on time every morning.

Whether in or out of the work setting, when we are open and pay attention, opportunities to connect, to grow, and to learn are everywhere — while waiting in line to pay for groceries, while driving our cars, or while standing by the coffee machine in the office. Finding fulfillment and satisfaction at work is vital to our health and our spirit. According to Suzuki Roshi, "On one side we are all fools. But when we realize this, we are enlightened." So Zen can be pretty enigmatic. It is actually okay to be a fool! If we don't sometimes play the fool, we cannot learn and grow and become more fully ourselves.

THE BENEFITS OF INTEGRATING
ZEN PRACTICE WITH YOUR WORK

C ompany Time is a series of one-day and weekend retreats that
I have been co-leading at Zen Center's Green Gulch Farm for
the past seven years. These retreats are for people interested in
integrating spiritual practice and work practice, for those looking
for ways to make their work more meaningful, more connected
to their deepest values, or for those considering some kind of
career or life change. I usually begin each retreat by stating that we
actually don't have anything to teach. Our role is to ask questions
and to provide a safe environment for slowing down, listening, and
speaking openly. We often announce that if we were to supply a
tape at the end of the retreats, it would be blank. The real teaching,
the real lessons, can only come from your experience. We will lose
ourselves if we aim for results or benefits. When we give up trying
to change or to improve we can open our hearts, and real change,
real benefits, become possible. Even though we don't aim for
results, integrating Zen practice with our work lives can bring
about a host of significant benefits.

In my role as CEO of a growing publishing company I often
find myself leading meetings and making presentations. In this
role I like to begin by looking ahead to what I hope to achieve and

understand more clearly. When the meeting or presentation is complete, what do I want to have addressed, what outcomes do I hope to realize? What are the benefits and the results to you as a participant in the meeting or as someone attending the presentation? My intention is to include and connect with each person. Since we (you as the reader and I) may be "meeting" here for the first time, let's begin, as I would in a meeting or presentation, at the end, with the anticipated outcomes. Here are what I perceive as the benefits of integrating Zen practice with your work:

- increased creativity

- improved listening and communication skills

- enhanced problem-solving skills

- the chance to build integrity and deepen relationships

- a way to build leadership and team-building skills

- increased work satisfaction

- improved focus and concentration

- increased appreciation for your life and your work

- the chance to develop entrepreneurial thinking and action

- a way to bring humor and joy into your work life

- the opportunity to contribute to a more connected, more sustainable world

Let's explore each of these benefits now.

Increased creativity. The aim of Zen practice is to develop a flexible, open mind. Slowing down and paying attention to your thinking and your body open new possibilities. Understanding that the world is not always what it seems fosters seeing problems and opportunities from a different perspective. This can be applied to problem solving, product development, and improving business systems.

Increased listening and communication skills. Mindfulness practice and deep listening are integral to Zen practice. You will learn the practice of deep listening, to yourself and to others. These skills can be applied to sales, team building, and general problem solving. Business ideas and business models start from paying attention to unfulfilled needs. When the mind is less busy and the ability to focus and concentrate is more developed you can communicate more clearly to people you work with, your customers, and your vendors. By shifting your focus and attention you build relationships as a way to improve outcomes and meet goals.

Enhanced problem-solving skills. Learn to embrace both a conventional viewpoint and an unconventional viewpoint of yourself and the world. Understand that time and space both exist and don't exist as we normally see them. Seeing through this lens, problems become opportunities. Meditation and Zen practice transform our focus so that we come to understand that our problems, difficulties, and challenges are actually our best friends and greatest teachers.

The chance to build integrity and deepen relationships. Slowing down and paying attention connects you to your deepest feelings and intentions, and the feelings and intentions of people in your workplace. Practicing right thinking, right speech, and right action (which we will learn more about in part 2) helps develop straightforward, open, and honest communication. By building integrity you deepen trust levels and connections with people around you.

A way to build leadership and team-building skills. Through practicing right speech and learning to bring the best out of others, our leadership skills are accentuated. The combination of self-knowledge, better listening skills, and heightened appreciation of the mystery of life makes for a more developed leader. Better relationships and cohesiveness come from improved listening and speech, and from actions becoming better aligned with deep beliefs and goals. Build creative and cohesive teams by clearer evaluation of your own and others' strengths and weaknesses, and by seeing other people as primarily focused on awakening their true natures.

Increased work satisfaction. As work becomes a context for the practice of awakening, it's transforming for yourself and for the people around you. Each moment becomes an opportunity to practice, to listen, and to be grateful for what we have. Mistakes and setbacks become opportunities.

Improved focus and concentration. Develop the ability both to focus on one project or object and to bring larger issues and strategies into focus. Improve the ability to concentrate and learn to cut through distractions. Learn to "stay close to yourself" by knowing in your bones what is truly important and by not getting caught by old patterns and habits.

Increased appreciation for your life and your work. As you clarify and soften your thinking, the context of your work shifts to become an integral part of your practice and your life. Appreciation arises as you reduce habitual thinking and actions. There is nothing but appreciation when you are living in the moment instead of being distracted by looking toward a past and future that don't really exist.

The chance to develop entrepreneurial thinking and action. Noticing and altering habitual patterns of thinking opens the way for a different quality of thought. With a taste of freedom from habitual thinking comes the ability to see and act with less hindrance. As you learn to trust yourself deeply, fear lessens and actions become more focused and affective. Increase your ability to move fearlessly and at the same time to evaluate the entire situation from several viewpoints, thus minimizing risk.

A way to bring humor and joy into your work life. Once we acknowledge how difficult it is to be alive, how difficult it can be to align our work lives with our deepest values, we can relax, smile, and laugh. What's the alternative? Wendell Berry once said, "Be joyful, though you have considered the alternatives."

The opportunity to contribute to a more connected, more sustainable world. Business has the potential to influence and change our world. Through integrating Zen practice with your work you can transform yourself and your workplace and effect positive change with your customers, vendors, other businesses, and other countries. Every person with whom you come into contact also connects with many people. The impact of one person or one business acting for the true benefit of others can have a transformative, inconceivable impact. The Tao-te Ching sums up these concepts well:

> *To obtain trust, put your trust in others.*
> *Take care! Speak only when it is essential.*
> *Then, when the work is done and the job is finished,*
> *Everyone will say that it happened naturally.*

UNFREEZING YOUR WORLD

After I had first lived at Tassajara for a year and a half, I was asked to leave and go to Green Gulch Farm, one of three locations that make up the San Francisco Zen Center. I was surprised, and not very happy, since I loved being at Tassajara and thought I was going to live there for several more years. I was particularly surprised to discover that I was being asked to go to Green Gulch Farm to be in charge of the draft horse farming project. Green Gulch had recently acquired a team of Percheron draft horses (each horse weighed about eighteen hundred pounds) with the intention of reviving the nearly forgotten practice of farming with horses as an environmental, social, and practical model.

I thought some terrible mistake had been made in choosing me for this job. Though I was quite athletic during high school and did spend some time on the horse in gymnastics, I had no experience at all with the four-legged kind. Not only did I have no experience with horses, I knew nothing about any of the practical abilities required to do this job — farming, carpentry, welding, and the numerous other skills required to farm with horses. I wondered if someone had misread my résumé.

Looking back, I think that my father, who had been an electrician and was always building things around the house when I was a child, kept me from learning physical, practical skills. His vision for me was that I would become a "professional," which he saw as having much higher status than a craftsperson or laborer, as he considered himself. After arriving at Green Gulch I discovered that I loved working with my hands, being physical each day, and working with these large, amazing animals.

Many years later, I asked Yvonne, who was a member of the group that had decided that it was time for me to leave Tassajara and go to Green Gulch why they had chosen me. Yvonne told me that she had been the key person in making this decision. She said that she knew because of the way I walked I would be good with the horses. That certainly clarified everything!

One of the first skills I needed to learn was welding. A variety of old horse equipment was scattered around the farm, but much of it was in need of repair. My welding teacher at Zen Center's Green Gulch Farm explained to me that the secret of welding is understanding that the world only appears to be frozen. The natural, actual state of the world is fluid. Welding is the process of applying heat to metals as a way of returning them to their natural, unfrozen condition. Once heated, metals become flexible and can be easily moved and shaped in whatever way we want.

My teacher continued to explain that welding can also teach us a great deal about work and life. Sometimes it looks as though we are confined to this body, in this place and this time. When we deeply pay attention to our lives, our world becomes unfrozen and less static. We can see that our lives and the world are actually fluid. We can see that our idea of time as moving from past to present to future is a false construct — something we create to help us get our bearings and to feel more comfortable. This very moment is completely fluid, containing the past as well as the future. It can be either terrifying or liberating to experience the fluidity of time.

As we loosen our habitual thinking, our view of who we are transforms and becomes more flexible and open: Who is this person, this self that we call me? Where did these hands, this body come from? As we loosen our conditioned thinking and views our relationship with work can be transformed. Once we have "unfrozen" our lives, our breathing and thinking become more spacious, and we can find true joy, peace, and freedom.

In welding we apply the heat of fire to transform metal. In our work and in our lives, we practice meditation, mindfulness, awareness, and compassion, and we experience the shortness and sacredness of life. This enables us to live fully in each moment, outside our usual conceptions of ourselves and the world.

Seeing the world as fluid might seem to be a rather mystical concept, but it is also a very practical one. Our bodies and minds are constantly in motion, changing, growing, healing, decaying, and dying. Our planet is primarily composed of hot, unstable liquid. We are reminded of this when we bathe in hot springs or when molten lava finds its way to the Earth's surface. And our world, our universe, is completely unknown and unfathomable. Can time really be explained rationally? What is the beginning and ending of time? The truth is that we have no idea where we come from or where we are going. How is it that we came to be born? How is it that breathing happens? These questions bridge the practical and the mystical. We can approach them solely from a rational or a mystical viewpoint, or we can engage and embrace both viewpoints simultaneously.

When we look closely we can see that the business world is also

quite fluid. At each moment billions of people are making decisions about what to buy and what to sell; they are making small
decisions and enormous decisions, for themselves, for their companies, for the government. The ebb and flow of this activity is as
fluid, as predictable, and as unpredictable as the liquid world
described by my welding teacher.

When we deeply pay attention, our work provides opportunities for tapping into this vast, mysterious, fluid world. Through our
work we can increase our understanding, healing, and growth, and
we can shape our world toward positive change. Our work connects the simple, mundane activities that we perform with our
larger place in our community and our world. Our work itself can
be the path we are seeking.

WORK: THE IMPOSSIBLE REQUEST

E arlier this year I attended a ceremony at the San Francisco Zen Center in which a new abbot, or spiritual leader, was being installed. I was one of six people chosen to ask the incoming abbot a question that he was to answer in public as part of the ceremony. The purpose of this exchange was to challenge and test the new abbot's wisdom and understanding and simultaneously to support and encourage him. The question that came to me was, "What is the impossible request your life makes of you?" The new abbot answered that his life was asking him "to keep my heart open, to the pains and sorrows, to the joy and well-being of everyone in my life, to not turn away from what was difficult but to turn toward it." I think that question and answer can be applied to our own lives and jobs.

What is the impossible request that your life asks of you? Stop for a moment and ask yourself that question, very slowly. Now slower. "What is the impossible request that my life makes of me?" Have you ever asked yourself this question? Don't have a clue what this means? That's okay. The question is more important than the answer. Just trust the question.

Your work and your life are impossible, imperfect, messy,

unanswerable. Your work and your life are precious, amazing, challenging, and incomprehensible. Is there any difference between these two, what is messy and what is precious? What if you accepted and appreciated your work and your life, just as they are, right now, without judgments and labels? Your work, and your life, if you are paying attention, present themselves as impossible requests, asking impossible things from you that are impossible to respond to.

Trust the questions. Trust what is difficult, unpredictable, and does not quite fit anywhere. There is no other place than right here, no other time than right now. There is no other question than this one — "What is the impossible request that my life asks of me?" In Zen there is a classic conversation, a koan, a dialogue between Bodhidharma, the founder of Zen, and Emperor Wu, the political head of China in the sixth century. Emperor Wu asks Bodhidharma, "What is the highest meaning of the holy truths?" Bodhidharma replies, "Empty, without holiness." The emperor asks, "Who is facing me?" Bodhidharma responds, "I don't know."

Without holiness, our work lives are empty. We write, we talk, we meet with people, we take out the trash. Work is one moment after another. But our work lives are precious and amazing. When asked who we are at work or how we came to be doing the work we do, the real answer, for most of us is, "I don't know." Our lives and our work are much like a koan, an impossible question whose purpose is to penetrate and deepen our understanding of our truth and the mysterious and mundane nature of our days.

Most of us have no idea how we came to do the work we are doing. Some people clearly choose their work. Others seem to be chosen by their work, and for many, work appears to be a result of a series of accidents. All three of these statements seem to describe how I came to be the founder of a greeting card publishing company. I can trace a series of choices that led me to this place. From another perspective it does feel as though there were a series of choices made, and that I just happened to be at the right place at the right time, on the receiving end of a constellation of decisions. Clearly my being in this role is the result of an amazing series of accidents and unexplainable events. My question continues, again and again — "What is the impossible request that my life asks of me?"

OUR HAPPINESS AND FREEDOM ARE
RIGHT HERE, RIGHT NOW

On my way to work on Christmas Eve morning I decided to stop at the local supermarket to buy some bagels to bring to the office. I went inside and was disappointed with the bagels I found in the bin. Having been a bread baker I could tell that they were not fresh, that they were probably a day old. I decided not to buy these bagels and instead to drive to a local bagel shop where the bagels would probably be fresher. As I was leaving the store I felt sad seeing the employees of the supermarket, looking bored and unhappy, restocking shelves and working the cash register.

I got into my car and burst out laughing at myself, thinking — how amazing — I'm leaving this store because I don't want day-old bagels and am about to drive ten minutes out of my way to Sausalito for freshly made bagels. How badly I am treating those poor day-old bagels, and how arrogant and insensitive I am being. What kind of Zen priest am I? Then I caught a glimpse of the wet, green hillsides surrounding me in the grocery store parking lot in beautiful Mill Valley, California. I thought of the sadness I sensed in the workers in the supermarket. I began to cry. Then I began to laugh. I realized how incredibly blessed I am. I started and manage a company that I love and care about. My kids are amazing human beings who each have the potential to bring peace and joy to the world. My wife loves me. I have clean air to breathe and good food to eat. And my main task for the day is to hand out bonus checks and gifts to employees at work this day before Christmas. In this moment I felt happy, blessed, and complete. And, yes, in the next moment I drove to Sausalito for fresh bagels.

Pai Chang was a Zen teacher in China during the ninth century. He always insisted on working each day as an integral part of his daily Zen practice. When he became old he continued this practice of working every day. At some point his students felt that he should stop working and hid his tools. In response he refused to eat and said, "A day of no work is a day of no food." This saying became a famous earmark of Zen practice and to this day work remains an integral part of it.

Zen Buddhism teaches that we suffer and feel pain because we want what we think we don't have or we don't want what we think we have. This suffering is caused by our mistaken belief that we are separate from other people and from the world. We suffer because we have been conditioned to think and believe that we have a real and solid identity, defined by our history, and that the future requires our constant concern and worry. Our thinking and conditioning about our history and the future prevents us from living right now, in this moment. It prevents us from expressing our true nature.

Zen provides a way to untangle these basic beliefs about the existence of a separate self and about there being any time but right now. Zen Buddhism is rooted in the belief that meditation practice, mindfulness practice, and work are in themselves expressions of freedom, and that these practices can be done anywhere, anytime, with the workplace being particularly conducive to them.

Zen teaches that our happiness and freedom are right here, right now. There is no need to go anywhere or do anything. Zen is a path and practice to transform suffering into peace and joy, to transform anxiety into calm and equanimity.

Buddha's insight about the cause of suffering and the path to end suffering has persevered and thrived for twenty-five hundred years. Zen Buddhism came into being about fifteen hundred years ago when the mystical Buddhist culture of India met the practical, work-oriented culture of China. Zen returned Buddhism to its roots, emphasizing meditation practice and, as Indian sage Bodhidharma, the founder of Zen, so eloquently stated, "experiencing the wisdom of the present moment, outside all scriptures and teachings."

Work has always played a central and critical role in Zen practice. There is a famous story about Dogen, the founder of Zen in Japan and perhaps the most revered teacher in all of Zen practice. Eight hundred years ago Dogen took the long and dangerous trip from Japan to China in search of a true Zen teacher. The first person he met was a Zen monk in his seventies whom Dogen was surprised to discover was the head cook in a large monastery. This monk had traveled several miles to buy some mushrooms for the evening meal. Dogen was excited to meet a Chinese Zen monk and invited him to spend the evening with him. When the monk said that he needed to return to the temple to make dinner, Dogen said that surely there must be others who could do the cooking and that an older monk didn't need to make the long trip back that evening. The monk laughed and said that it was his responsibility and his practice to oversee the cooking of the meals. He said that this foreigner clearly did not understand that Zen practice was not separate from the act of work. Dogen was moved by this conversation and by the spirit of this monk. In another famous Zen dialogue the student asks, "What is the essence of Zen?" The teacher responds, "Chopping wood and carrying water." Zen practice emphasizes simplicity and action. In Zen practice, work itself by its very nature both allows us to express our true nature and provides the ground for awakening.

BEFORE AWAKENING, WORK IS JUST WORK; AFTER AWAKENING, WORK IS JUST WORK

I was recently interviewed by a reporter for a national Buddhist publication who was doing a story about how business leaders with spiritual backgrounds deal with difficulty and adversity in their businesses. I recounted a variety of challenging situations that I have encountered over the years, including not having money to pay the payroll, being millions of dollars in debt during our Internet phase, letting go of twelve people in one day, having shipments of product arrive from China packed incorrectly, and employees either not showing up for work or resigning for a variety of personal reasons. In hearing about these tales the reporter wanted to know how I reacted, how I used my years of Zen training. Over and over I responded that I just did my best to tell the truth and to be present, open, and honest. I did whatever I could to take care of the people and directly meet the situations I faced. The reporter kept digging deeper, and finally a bit exasperated, he asked, "How is what you do any different from what any business leader does who is just trying to be kind?" I responded, "That's right. That's all I'm doing, just trying to be kind." It seemed I had let him down.

There is a Zen expression, "Before we are enlightened, mountains are mountains and rivers are rivers. Once enlightened, mountains are no longer just mountains and rivers are no longer just rivers.

After enlightenment, mountains are mountains and rivers are rivers." It is also true that before we are awakened, work is just work. Once awakened, work is no longer just work. After awakening, work once again is just work.

Before we begin walking our spiritual path, before we begin to pay attention, problems are just problems, we are caught by failure and success, trapped by our desires. Our lives are like leaves on an autumn stream — we are tossed about, out of control, going from one difficult situation to another. We are completely controlled by the patterns and habits learned over a lifetime.

Regular meditation and Zen practice give us an experience of seeing beyond our usual perspective of ourselves and the world. We are no longer always caught up in our ideas and judgments. We see how our desires and cravings affect us, and we become more aware of the shortness of our lives. We develop insight into our conditioned habits and learn how not to be continually fooled by these habits. We see the ways we have created walls and barriers that protect us but also hinder us. Awakening is seeing that we have constructed these barriers and also that they don't really exist. From the perspective of this awakening, everything appears different. Once awakened to this viewpoint, we experience everything differently, and at the same time we still are subject to our own habits, struggles, and patterns. We still need food and air and love. We understand and accept our barriers, limitations, and habits, and begin the long hard work of understanding ourselves more fully, helping others, and transforming our society and our world. In Zen practice this is called having a "way-seeking mind," as we discussed above, or a "beginner's mind." With this mind, we enter our lives and the world, embracing both the ordinary and the mystical. In our daily lives there is no choice but to get up, brush our teeth, and go to work.

Zen practice has a way of blurring the lines between what is practical and what is mystical, what is ordinary and what is sacred. The act of work is considered practical and mystical, both ordinary and sacred — no difference. Most of us have no trouble seeing work as practical and ordinary. But, we ask, what is so mystical and sacred about work? What is mystical about going to meetings, writing emails, managing cash flow, and writing business plans?

From an ordinary viewpoint, we are in control. Things are just as they appear. Each day the sun rises and sets. We are born, we grow old, and we die. We need to make money and pay taxes. Our attitudes and beliefs and the attitudes and beliefs of others are difficult to change. Work is something we must do to make money. We want to work as little as possible and make the most money possible. We can't be our full selves at work. We work for money, benefits, free time, control, or power.

From a mystical point of view, we are not in control. We see ourselves and everyone else as divine creations. Things are not at all as they appear. Time just appears to be predictable, moving from one moment to the next. In actuality time is fluid. It is an illusion that we are stuck in this time; and it is an illusion that we are stuck in this body. Whose body is this? Who is it that is breathing? Do we own our breath; do we own this body? Who is the "I" thinking these thoughts? From a mystical viewpoint, our work is sacred, an expression of our deepest intention. Work is an opportunity to practice mindfulness, generosity, and compassion.

EMBRACING THE ORDINARY AND THE MYSTICAL

In Zen practice we embrace the mystical and the ordinary — we are in control, and we are not in control. Everything is ordinary *and* mystical — we need to see both sides; when we see just one side we have an incomplete vision. We can learn from the simplest things. Cleaning toilets is just cleaning toilets, and it can also be a mystical activity.

In Zen practice it is said that it is a mistake, a delusion, to think that we wash dishes or clean toilets because they are dirty. Instead, we wash dishes and clean toilets in order to wash dishes and clean toilets. Our idea of clean and dirty can get in the way of the practice of just being fully present to the meeting of the rag, the cleanser, the white ceramic bowl, and our body and mind. The goal is not simply to clean the toilet.

THE GOAL: NO GOAL

In Zen practice our goal is to not have a goal. Zen is not about improving or changing. Zen practice is precisely that — a practice: meditation practice, study, and work. The practice itself is the goal, and nothing more. The practice of Zen is to fully be ourselves, to be fully present to what is right in front of us, not to add anything on to ourselves. A cartoon shows two Zen monks sitting in meditation. One monk leans over and asks the other, "What happens next?" The other monk replies, "Nothing; this is it." It is much the same in our lives and in our work. Nothing happens next; this is it!

We can change the usual context of our work lives in several ways:

1. *We can fully accept and own where we are.* We see that our time at work is no different from any other time in our lives. We can accept that it is no accident that we are where we

are, that we have chosen to be where we are, and that we are doing what we should be doing (this doesn't mean we will always be here doing this. In fact, it is clear that we will definitely not always be here doing this).

2. *We can be fully ourselves at work.* We can begin with the assumption that we can be fully ourselves at work. We do not check our personalities at the door — certainly not the best part of our personalities. We can be just who we are, no different from how we are with our family and friends or how we are when we are our deepest and most real selves. What stops us from doing this?

3. *Work can be an opportunity to develop ourselves.* We see that work can be an opportunity to pay attention, to practice mindfulness, to practice honesty and integrity, to learn about ourselves through interacting with people, to help others through the activity of work, to question and loosen the conditioned assumptions about our being separate.

4. *Work itself is an expression of our true nature.* We understand that work itself is an expression of the mysterious and mundane nature of our lives. We may not always see or experience our work in this way, but having had a taste, we know it to be true.

TEN OX-HERDING PICTURES

In Zen literature there is a well-known series of pictures that depict and compare a person's search for an ox with the stages of spiritual practice. The first picture is called "searching for the ox," signifying taking the first steps on the spiritual path. The tenth and last picture is called "returning to the marketplace," signifying having gone through all nine stages of development and then returning to the world. It is significant that the tenth and most "advanced" stage of spiritual life is seen as going back into the life of work. The most advanced practice is the invisible one of living a spiritual life in the ordinary world of work, where "chopping wood and carrying water" might also be just "going to meetings and talking on the telephone."

For most of us spiritual practice and the development of our work lives don't come in ten clear steps or stages. Each day we have the opportunity to develop our spiritual life, and each day we have the opportunity to return to the marketplace by integrating and bringing our spiritual life to work, or perhaps by bringing our work to our spiritual life.

THE FIRST THING,
THE MOST IMPORTANT THING

When I lived at Green Gulch Farm my life consisted of farming with horses, milking cows, caring for chickens, participating in the regular daily meditation schedule, and helping to take care of Harry Roberts. Harry was in his late sixties, and his health was failing. He had lived at Green Gulch as a young man, working as a cowboy and tending cattle. He was trained as a Yurok Indian shaman and was one of the most knowledgeable people in the world regarding California native plants. The name I gave my company, Brush Dance, comes from a story that Harry once told.

I used to help Harry with his errands by driving him around in his old yellow Ford pickup truck. He instructed me to use the brakes as little as possible, as a way of extending their life. As his health declined we drove less often, and he spent more time in bed. I did some shopping, often cooked him meals, and would empty the container of urine that he kept under his bed. Harry sometimes said that the first thing we must do if we want to find real happiness and freedom is to stop the busyness in our minds. "This is not the most important thing, but the first thing," he would say. To do this we must find regular time to stop and practice meditation. Nothing fancy is needed. A simple black cushion is fine. "Just go sit on a rock or a log," Harry often said. We stop the busyness by paying attention to our thoughts, our emotions, and our bodies. We learn not to be controlled by our thoughts — we don't stop the thoughts; we stop the busyness. Take the time to slow down, to accomplish nothing. Just sit. This is the first thing.

The next task is to find your song. We each have a purpose for being born. We each have unique talents that can be cultivated. We each have a song within us. Harry sometimes said that a basic difference between the Native American culture and our culture today is that Native Americans believed that each person was born for a reason and that everyone has a unique gift, a unique offering. The role of parents is to provide opportunities for each child to discover their gift. This stands in contrast to the values often expressed and taught in today's culture in which parents and teachers emphasize success, money, and power without including the development of a child's innate talents and abilities.

Harry advised that one way to discover your unique gift is to think about what you most liked to do, what you were most drawn to when you were a child. Try to think back to when you were three or four years old. What kinds of activities brought you joy? What were you drawn to do? What really made you happy? Harry describes that when he was very young he loved to be around plants and watch things grow. Some part of him knew that this would be his life's work. He went on to become a farmer and agronomist. He owned and ran a nursery and later in his life designed the botanical gardens at the University of California in Berkeley.

What did you most like to do as a child? Was it playing the piano, reading books, fixing things, throwing a baseball, or making people laugh? Look for your particular gift. We might be quite elated or quite disappointed with this approach. From this perspective we see that many things about us are unique, and we think about how we can apply these to our work. We recognize how complex our lives are and realize that we must make certain decisions, that we can satisfy some parts of ourselves but not others. If we are good with numbers, then perhaps we should be an accountant or math teacher. If we are good with words we might consider writing, editing, or teaching.

From a wider perspective we see that we all have some deep purpose in life, and our goal is to uncover this purpose and express it in our work. We are aware that our work serves a higher purpose and that it is important to discover our true calling. Discovering what is in our heart and integrating this with our work can be an important part of a spiritual path.

Zen practice offers us an even wider perspective. From an awakened point of view we realize that whatever we are doing we are singing our song. It is impossible not to. We understand that there can be no success or failure. We are perfect just as we are. At this level we can fully accept and be ourselves. We can appreciate the preciousness of life. At the same time we pay close attention to our body and mind, ready to respond to whatever might come our way. As Suzuki Roshi was fond of saying, "You are perfect just as you are, and you could use some improvement." None of these perspectives is better or more true than the others. Each is important to understand and to hold. Discovering our song and learning to sing it is a lifelong, ongoing process.

THAT DARN TAIL

"It is like a buffalo that passes through a window. Its head, horns, and legs pass through. Why can't its tail pass through as well?"

Though short and mysterious, this is one of my favorite Zen stories. It was written in China, during the pinnacle of Chinese Zen, more than a thousand years ago and is part of a collection of forty-eight stories called *The Gateless Barrier*. Studying Zen stories is a way to study and understand our lives. What does this story mean? What does it have to do with our lives and our jobs? What can we learn from this simple, enigmatic story? How can we apply what we learn?

One of the images I have when I read this story is watching the births of my son and my daughter. As they were born into this world, I watched as they passed through the opening in their mother — first the head, then the body, then the legs, then the feet. Yet a part of them was still connected to the world before we are born, the world that exists before birth, a place beyond words and beyond form. In many ways this connection, this tiny tail, felt more vital than this human existence; it felt as if this connection to a world beyond what we usually view informed and colored everything else.

This story also brings forth the ideas I have about work as spiritual practice. In our thinking minds it is as though work and spiritual practice are two separate, competing ideas that do not fit together in a neat or explainable package. There is always a sense of something missing, something not being completely right, completely whole, or completely understandable. That darn tail! Our minds want easy, neat, explainable solutions — the buffalo should just pass through the window, tail and all. Or we ask, Why is this buffalo going through a window in the first place?

Facing difficulty is the starting point for integrating Zen practice and business practice. Just as our lives are difficult, business is difficult. Starting a business, finding capital, finding and managing employees, sales, operations, finance, production, and manufacturing are all fraught with difficulties and challenges. There is always more to learn, more to accomplish, and more to understand.

We exacerbate difficulties in business by wanting things to be different from how they are, by wanting things to be neat and to fit our images of how we want things to be or how they are supposed to be. Yes, there is a paradox here. Our jobs are often to make things different from how they are, to increase sales, to provide better service, to educate, to increase efficiency, and so on. But if we are always focused on change, on getting results, we can be distracted from being attentive, being present to what is right in front of us. Our habits and patterns get in the way. Once we recognize and accept difficulty as a part of our business life, we see how not accepting what is right in front of us increases the difficulty. Once we experience the possibility of accepting and using difficulty we can begin to use business as a path to our own awakening.

Zen practice is based on facing and entering the difficulties and problems in our lives. Immeasurable pain and suffering are caused by business leaders not accepting and dealing with the difficulties of business — covering up losses, not facing emotional shortcomings, hiding environmental dangers. The habit of wanting to look good and successful and not wanting to face difficulty is particularly dangerous for business leaders. The pattern of focusing on one person's or one group's interest at the expense of other people and other groups leads to instability and to the creation of additional suffering.

When our work lives are in crisis or when we are extremely unhappy with our work, we try hard to end the difficulty. When we work through the crisis we feel relieved for the moment. Usually this feeling of satisfaction and acceptance doesn't last long. When our jobs are going well, when we are not in pain, we forget about the difficulty and take our work for granted. We usually do not appreciate when business goes well. It can be a challenge to appreciate our health, the health of our business, someone's smile, the flowers outside our office, or the blue sky.

A paradox of Zen practice is that when we accept and fully embrace pain and difficulty, the path of joy and deep satisfaction opens to us. By being fully present we can get out of our own way: effort without effort. When we remove the images we have of a perfect, difficulty-free work life and actually start to appreciate the difficulties, our work lives are transformed.

WALKING THE PATH

WALKING THE PATH

M y twenty-year-old son recently said to me, "Look at you, Dad. You are old, short, balding, and have crooked teeth. You have the responsibility of caring for children, and you run a business and own a home. I don't think I want to be anything like you." I felt tremendous love and affection from and for my son. I could see that he was struggling to understand his own future and the decisions and choices that would confront him as he developed. I felt proud to see my son searching and questioning. What is real freedom? What is responsibility? How do our ideas get in the way? How do we act freely, effectively, beyond success or failure, free of fear, free from hindrance?

I pointed out that he probably would, unfortunately, look like me when he got to be my age. About the responsibility of having children and running a business, I asked him, "What's the alternative? Do you think that freedom means not having responsibility, not making difficult choices?"

Being alive is difficult. Having a body and a mind is difficult. Being ourselves at work is difficult. Even when we are happy, we still sense some separation, knowing that this happiness cannot last forever. There is no avoiding pain, suffering, sickness, old age, and death. We make life even more difficult by not accepting these facts and running away from difficulty and pain and responsibility. We develop amazing strategies for avoiding pain that lead to habitual ways of thinking and acting. Recognizing this, we can get a glimpse of our own part in creating suffering and see the possibility of joy, peace, and freedom.

Difficulty and discomfort exist. They are caused by the fact of being alive and by our awareness of being separate. It is possible to end difficulty and discomfort by fully realizing that we are not separate. These are the first three of what in Buddhism are called the Four Noble Truths, the historical Buddha's insight into the nature of difficulty and how to attain real freedom. The fourth of these Noble Truths is the path toward ending difficulty and discomfort, called the Eightfold Path: right view, right thinking, right speech, right action, right livelihood, right diligence, right mindfulness, and right concentration. The word *right* more literally means upright or straight, not bent or crooked. It means beneficial. Through your experience you discover what is beneficial and what is not.

Zen practice is based on your experience. The Buddha and all Zen teachers are clear on this point. There is no truth outside your experience. All the tools and materials you need to find real happiness and satisfaction in your work, and in your life, are right at hand. Your pain and difficulty, your joy and happiness, your strengths and weaknesses, your failures and success are all the "compost" for you to use in growing the garden that is you.

This recognition, this radical insight into completely accepting who we are and where we are in our lives is the starting point for integrating our spiritual practice and our work practice. Even to use these words is missing the point when we begin to see that there is no difference between our work lives and our spiritual practice — our work is our spiritual practice; our spiritual practice is our work.

Integrating Zen practice with your work is more than an idea; it is actually something that you can *do*. The Eightfold Path provides specific ways, specific practices to bring the principles and values of Zen into your work. This was the path to awakening described by the Buddha:

- Uncovering your approach: right view

- What are you thinking? right thinking

- Paying attention: right mindfulness

- It's what you say: right speech

- It's what you do: right action

- It's your work: right livelihood

- Staying with it: right diligence

- Staying focused: right concentration

In the following chapters we will look at each of these practices in depth.

UNCOVERING YOUR APPROACH:
RIGHT VIEW

My cousin Gary is a successful businessman living on the East Coast. He works hard and with intensity, is prone to high blood pressure, and feels concerned about his heart and overall health. He asked me if I thought that meditation practice might be useful in improving his health, and I told him I thought it might. He decided to fly out to spend a weekend at Zen Center's Green Gulch Farm.

A good friend of mine, Norman Fischer, was abbot at the Zen Center at that time. I asked Norman to look out for Gary and to welcome him if they happened to cross paths. Gary told me that when he first arrived at Green Gulch he met Norman in the parking lot. Norman was very friendly and welcoming. Then he said to Gary, "If you think that being at Green Gulch for the weekend is going to help you, you are wasting your time." Gary told me later that he was not very encouraged by this statement. Norman had gone on to say, "Zen practice is about changing your life, changing how you view yourself and the world, and requires much more than a weekend."

The practice of right view can be applied to ourselves and to our work. We each approach our work lives with a variety of essential

motivations and from different perspectives. You may be passionate about a particular activity or feel that you have a talent that
needs expression. You might be driven by the fear of failure or the
fear of not being able to provide for your family. You might be
motivated by a strong desire to succeed, to achieve certain goals.
You may want to make positive change in your community. Your
work may reflect your sense of identity and how you perceive
yourself and your environment. You might feel a gap between what
you want to do and what you are actually doing. You may feel a gap
between how you experience your work activity and your image of
what you want your work activity to be.

Zen practice provides a container that is wide enough to contain
all these possible motivations and to place them in a larger
framework — the framework of practice or of awakening. From
this perspective our work becomes a vehicle for working on our
lives. All our passions, desires, and fears provide information and
can be used in understanding and developing all aspects of our
lives, inside and outside our jobs.

From the perspective of right view, some kinds of activities
help us to feel comfortable, centered, and satisfied. Others cause us
to feel uncomfortable, agitated, and needy. Right view means paying attention to the activities, people, and situations that bring out
the best in us and the activities that bring out our worst. In Zen we
speak about right view as watering the seeds of wholesomeness
and not watering the seeds that are unwholesome. (*Wholesome* is
defined as activities that lead us to peace, freedom, and awakening;
unwholesome activities lead to suffering and craving and take us
away from our true nature.)

Right view is seeing how we hold on to perceptions and attitudes when they are no longer accurate or useful. It is developing

WALKING THE PATH

our understanding of how we create suffering. We unintentionally build walls around ourselves, either for protection or just out of habit. We don't see things as they are but as we want them to be or through the distortion of our needs or habits.

Business is very simple. Pay attention to and move toward what works, what meets the needs of your customers or constituents. See a need and find a way to meet this need. Brush Dance, for example, is a very simple business. We make greeting cards, and we sell them to stores. We need to sell enough cards, at a price higher than they cost to produce, to support the overhead of running a business — what could be simpler?

From another perspective Brush Dance is an extremely complicated affair, requiring hiring and managing employees, developing licensing agreements with artists and authors, managing cash flow and inventory, building channels of distribution, using software, accounting, and fulfillment systems, and on and on. Brush Dance takes products from the conception stage and orchestrates the production, warehousing, sales, and fulfillment of hundreds of products, which are produced in China, Korea, and throughout the United States. Our customers range from individuals purchasing on the Internet to major retail chains.

A major turning point for Brush Dance was seeing that from a strategic point of view, it is not a greeting card or gift company at all. Though we make greeting cards and gifts, what distinguishes Brush Dance from other card companies is that all our products combine words and images; and even more precisely, all our products contain spiritual or inspirational content. Realizing that we are a spiritual products company and not just a card company has transformed the business — the way we create products and how we view our channels of distribution. Operating a spiritual

65

products business is very different from running a greeting card business.

This point becomes even clearer if we examine the Brush Dance mission statement:

> The Brush Dance mission is to increase awareness, understanding, and compassion by combining powerful words and extraordinary art. Our products reflect our commitment to enhancing the quality of life, bridging the alternative and the mainstream, the sacred and the ordinary. We pursue this ideal by creating products that resonate in a deep way with our customers. We also express this mission in the way we conduct our business — through cultivating open, honest, and caring relationships with artists, authors, designers, and suppliers.

The practice of right view is going beyond ideas to the heart of things — to the heart of your life and to the heart of your work. It is paying attention to what is most important at this moment. It is asking and being aware of the question, What does this moment ask of me?

I recently found myself in the midst a difficult situation with one of my sales representatives. Marsha had been a Brush Dance representative for more than twelve years, and we had also become friends. Though she had previously been one of our top-performing representatives, her sales had declined in recent years, and we mutually decided to make some changes by cutting back her territory. Though I thought we were clear when we made these changes, I found out that Marsha was upset with me, not because of the decisions but because of how we each viewed the process and our relationship. After a few uncomfortable emails, I decided to call her. I realized that though the business decisions were awkward, they were not the heart of the problem. I told Marsha that I cared about her and our friendship, and I apologized for anything I might have done to let her down during this difficult transition. Changing my view of this situation and making myself vulnerable transformed the situation. My decision to expose my feelings and awkwardness allowed Marsha and me to meet, understand each other, and maintain, and perhaps develop, our friendship, as well as keep the door open to our business relationship.

We have ideas about what we need and also about what is needed in our business. Often many of these ideas are based on habits and patterns that have little to do with the situation at hand. Often they prevent us from seeing what is really needed. Our ideas can be based on seeing things from a narrow or self-centered perspective and not seeing the situation clearly. We have to learn, through our experience, what views nourish us and which ones take us further away from what we truly want.

It is no accident that the practice of right view was the first of the Eightfold Path as taught by the Buddha. It is the practice of assessing our own starting point, investigating the complexity of our motivations, and exploring the depths of our intentions. It requires looking directly and clearly into our habits and patterns, of seeing where we are stuck. Our own worldview shapes our reality, how we see ourselves, how we see others, how we see our work and our life. A famous Zen saying is "Complete awakening is easy, just stop picking and choosing; give up labeling right and wrong, good and bad."

From one point of view there are right views, and there are wrong views. From an awakened perspective there are no right or wrong views. Right view is not being influenced by preconceived ideas — that is, being able to see and feel clearly, without being stuck or attached to a particular opinion. This requires being fully present. When we develop this kind of awareness, it can sharpen our focus and allow us to make decisions and choices with greater clarity and authority. The right view, of not being attached to our own ideas, gives us some distance from the situation at hand, providing a unique and powerful perspective.

At the same time, we must acknowledge that we live in the human world. Of course we have views. Our views, passions, and opinions are important. How do we pay attention to and understand our views without becoming stuck to a particular way of seeing the world? How can we express our views in such a way that we are not being one-sided but rather helping others to understand and loosen their ideas that might be harmful or getting in the way? How can we be fully present and fully respond to whatever situation might confront us? There is a great quote by Nietzsche, which Brush Dance recently published as a greeting card: "It is hard enough to remember my opinions without also having to remember my reasons for them."

The essence of right view is paying attention. Notice how your body feels when you arrive at work, when you talk on the phone, when you are in meetings. Notice your state of mind as you prepare to work, as you engage in the activities of your day. Practice seeing yourself and your work from other people's perspectives. Try seeing yourself through the eyes of people you most admire and through the eyes of those you least admire. Regularly ask others for their open feedback about your work and your place in the work world. Inquire, with an open mind.

QUESTIONS FOR DAILY PRACTICE

- How does your state of mind affect what you do?

- How does what you do affect your state of mind?

- What is your most basic approach to work: fear, greed, helping others, a need for love, a need to feel competent or successful?

- How would you describe your purpose in life?

- Which of these is predominant over others? How do these approaches vary?

- What work activities give you energy?

- What work activities drain your energy?

- Where do you feel stuck? What situations and people encourage you to feel stuck?

- Where do you feel open? What situations and people encourage you to feel open?

- What people and work activities help you to see outside your usual patterns and habits?

- Who do you help most at work and in what ways?

- Who helps you the most?

WHAT ARE YOU THINKING?
RIGHT THINKING

When my mother became ill and it appeared that she was not going to live much longer, she sold her home in Florida and came to live with me and my family in northern California. After many weeks of seeing a variety of doctors, we learned that she had developed a lung infection and did not have long to live. The doctors suggested that I bring her home and make her comfortable. Hearing this news, my mother was both sad and relieved and made the decision to give herself over to the process of dying.

My wife and I gave my mother our bedroom, thinking that she would want to stay in a quiet space, away from the activity of our two young children. Instead, she gravitated to the center of activity, and we found that she wanted to stay on our living room couch. She became the center of attention, and my wife and children all took part in taking care of her.

One afternoon I prepared one of her favorite treats — a milk shake made with fresh fruit. When I brought it to her she had a puzzled, uncomfortable expression on her face. "What are you thinking?" she asked. "I'm trying to die, and you are bringing me milk shakes!" "It's fine with me if you die, Mom," I answered. "I just want you to die healthy."

Issues of life and death, in our personal and business lives, can help to clarify, sharpen, and sometimes allow our thinking to become both more spacious and focused. When we are able to get out of our own way, our thinking can bubble up from deep and mysterious places. Our thoughts may surprise us. We may think of things and respond to situations in ways that are new and imaginative.

Thinking is our internal speech. Our minds are extremely skillful at this art. Observing and paying attention to our thinking is very important at work. Our thinking allows our speech and our actions to be clear, or it can get in the way.

You can apply several practices associated with right thinking to your work (and your life). Ask yourself the following questions:

1. *What am I sure of?* You see that someone in your office is unhappy, and you think it is related to something you have done or said, but you're not sure. How can you know without asking? Are you sure that your new product idea serves a need? Are you sure that your strategy plays into the existing strengths of your team? Asking these questions doesn't mean constantly doubting yourself; rather it is a regular reminder to be clear about what you think, about the assumptions you are making. This question is a tool to help you pay attention.

In today's rapidly changing work environment there is not much we can be sure of. Through practicing with this question we simultaneously sharpen our own consciousness and focus our awareness on changes in our environment. In all businesses our leaders and workers change, technology constantly changes, our competition changes, and the needs of our customers change. What are you sure of?

I have an agreement with my key managers that we don't make

assumptions about how we are feeling in relation to one another. If I notice that a manager seems unhappy or is short-tempered, I express what I'm seeing and feeling and inquire about what is happening. I've learned that making assumptions about others' experiences and feelings is almost always counterproductive and can lead to a lack of fluid communication.

2. *What am I really doing?* This question will clarify the purpose of your activity and help keep you focused and present. What am I really doing with my life? What am I really doing in my work? What is really important to me? How does this activity connect to my larger purpose? What is at the heart of this strategy? What am I really doing today at work?

This can be a powerful practice, again with applications to your internal development and to the development of your work focus and performance. This question and practice require that you keep coming back to the central question of your activity, your thinking, and your life.

3. *Is this kind of thinking a habit?* Much of our thinking is the same old story, over and over. Notice the story. Notice the things you think over and over that may actually have little to do with the situation. Habitual thinking can act as a drag in our lives and our work. This question helps you pay attention to your thinking. The patterns tend to stay the same; only the players and the situations change.

I have recently realized that the product-development process at Brush Dance has not changed to align with the changes in our rategy. Our habit is to develop products that ookstores and card stores. Though we now customers are major retailers we have not way that we think about, plan, and execute our product development. Changing these habits does not come easily. The skills required, and perhaps the people required, are different. The schedules for developing products need to be revised. We need to find different manufacturing sources in order to lower our costs, since larger customers require steeper discounts.

4. *Is this thinking cultivating understanding?* Pay attention to your thinking. Are your thoughts causing confusion and anxiety, or are they helping you to feel clearer, more loving, and more compassionate? Can you water the seeds of clarity and love and not water the seeds of anxiety? Can you water the seeds of creativity and energy and not water the seeds of doubts and confusion?

How well do you understand your customers and your business? How do you think about meeting the needs of your customers? Do you actually pay attention to your own thinking and give yourself and others the time to appreciate and examine your thoughts?

Our minds want to attach names and labels to everything. We tend to judge everything as good or bad, rich or poor, weak or strong, honest or dishonest, successful or unsuccessful. In business we are taught to quantify everything. When I was enrolled in the New York University MBA program I had a marketing class, the thrust of which was that everything needs to be quantified — *everything!* Once I figured out that this was the basic assumption of this class, I had an easy time succeeding. I discovered that it was easy to quantify everything. It was quite useful, and at the same time I was aware of the limitations of this approach.

Even in Zen practice our minds want to quantify and judge: How is my meditation practice? Where do I stand in relation to others? How am I doing following my breath? and on and on. We all want to look good and avoid looking bad; we all want to look smart and avoid looking dumb; we all want to look strong and avoid looking weak. We are all in the same lot as human beings — our bodies and minds are very fragile, we live in an unexplainable world in which most things are beyond our control, and we will all succumb to old age, sickness, and death. Our ideas about good and bad are a flimsy way to try to make sense of the world, to have at least a sense of control.

Our lives and our businesses are filled with paradox. As leaders, managers, and employees we want to be decisive. We must do our research, make decisions, and move forward confidently. At the same time life and business decisions are fraught with unknowns. If we are overconfident we may fall into the trap of not being careful enough or of not listening enough. If we move slowly, we may look carefully but not move quickly and confidently enough.

A critical aim of Zen practice and of business practice is to develop a flexible mind, a mind that can hold a variety of views — completely accepting of who we are and our abilities and at the same time working to grow and change, feeling complete and comfortable with circumstances just as they are and simultaneously working to make improvements. We learn to hold what appears to be opposing traits: simultaneously being confident and open to change; being strong and being vulnerable; trusting ourselves and trusting others. We also learn to feel accepting and comfortable with our own incompleteness and lack of comfort. Instead of wanting things to be different, we understand that things are what they are. And, of course, we continue to strive for a deeper understanding of our lives, our business, and our practice.

If you think you are a good parent or a good businessperson, you are caught by the label, by the judgment and the belief that time and our lives are stagnant and can be measured. In reality, all that exists is the present moment. At the same time we must clearly look at and learn from the past and plan meticulously for the future. And simultaneously we must look with open, fresh eyes for what the next moment may bring.

Pay attention to your thinking at different times of your workday. Notice how your thinking affects how you feel. Notice how the way you feel and the way you look at things affect your thinking. Notice how your thinking and feelings interact. Speak openly with your teacher or mentor about your thoughts. Get to know your thinking; become friends with it. Notice how your thinking affects your energy and your work and how your energy and your work influence your thinking.

QUESTIONS FOR DAILY PRACTICE

- How would you describe the quality of your thinking, right now, in general, at different times during your workday?

- How does your thinking affect how you feel?

- What is the relationship between your thinking and the quantity and quality of your work?

- Who are you when you are not thinking?

- How does thinking influence your speech and your actions?

PAYING ATTENTION:
RIGHT MINDFULNESS

I recently had dinner at a restaurant in San Francisco with a good friend of mine. She was the original manager of this restaurant and now acts as a consultant, helping to guide the management team.

Walking into this restaurant with my friend was a lesson for me in the practice of mindfulness in a business setting. Though we were merely going out for a casual dinner, I could see her carefully looking at details. As soon as we entered, my friend turned to me and pointed out that the shades above the large windows that look out on the San Francisco Bay were pulled down at different lengths. She was not happy about this. She also felt that the way we were greeted by the hostess was not nearly as friendly and welcoming as it should have been in this setting. She went on to tell me about the essential role the hostess plays, both as the first contact that people have in entering the restaurant and in controlling the flow of seating (and thus how this person directly affects the restaurant's revenue). I could see her rating each of the waiters and busboys on their level of professionalism and friendliness and by their presentation and how they provided excellent service while staying out of the customers' way. When dessert was served my friend was not happy with the size of the portions, explaining that portions this large are unnecessary and drive up costs. As a mentor of mine often says, "Take care of the details, and the big picture will take care of itself."

Right mindfulness is the basis of all Zen practice. The word *mindfulness* literally means "remembering." It is the practice of paying attention to what keeps you present and in the moment and of not directing your attention toward what takes you away from the present. Mindfulness can be practiced anytime during your workday, whether you are alone, with others, or in the midst of an intense discussion or negotiation. There are several aspects to Zen mindfulness practice — attention to body and mind, mindfulness of others, and nourishing others through attention, understanding, and transformation. Let's explore them now.

ATTENTION TO BODY AND MIND

Mindfulness begins when you pay attention to your breathing, your thoughts and emotions, and your entire body. You can do this in meditation practice, with your family, or while working. Notice your breathing while talking on the phone. Notice your chest and back while in a business meeting. When walking, try paying attention to your feet contacting the floor. When sitting at the computer pay attention to your posture, to your lower back, to your shoulders. Notice how your breathing affects your posture. Sometimes just sitting up straight, putting energy into your posture, can alter your breathing and shift the way you feel.

MINDFULNESS OF OTHERS

When we are mindful of others, we are focused on helping them to be fully present just by being fully present ourselves. Watch the body language of the people you work with. Working as a team requires that we understand how other members of the team function — their jobs and skills as well as emotional and spiritual strengths and weaknesses.

In the movie *Groundhog Day,* Bill Murray is stuck in a day that repeats over and over. I've always felt that this is a movie about the practice of mindfulness. At first the character played by Murray is completely self-centered. He reacts to this experience of each day repeating in annoyance and anger. In particular he gets angry with people who keep doing the exact same things, repeating their mistakes and habits. At some point he begins just to notice what people do, without becoming impatient. Then he sees that by really paying attention to the people around him he can understand and make real connections with them. By connecting with others he develops a renewed appreciation of his own life and begins to achieve many of the things that had eluded him previously.

NOURISHING OTHERS THROUGH ATTENTION, UNDERSTANDING, AND TRANSFORMATION

Expressing your appreciation for others can have a major impact on the well-being and performance of your business. Many studies have shown that one of the key motivators for people at work is feeling appreciated and having a clear understanding of how each person's actions contribute to the overall results of the company. By giving other people our attention we can help them to discover their own ease and vibrancy. At Brush Dance we recently began giving a monthly "above and beyond" award to an employee whose actions were above and beyond what is expected. Just paying attention to people in this way can help build trust and improve performance.

In addition, by paying close attention to ourselves, to others, and to the situation we increase our understanding. Mindfulness practice and understanding are closely linked. The more we pay attention to our bodies and minds, the more we pay attention to others, the more we develop understanding. With mindfulness practice you begin to become less self-centered and more centered on seeing yourself and the world as they are.

Finally, through attention to ourselves, to others, and our situation and by deepening our understanding, we can then transform our thinking and transform our situations. Problems can be transformed into opportunities. Is there any difference between a problem and an opportunity? Who decides? What influences how we see and label our situation?

Zen practice teaches us that all fear and anxiety come from not seeing things as they are. We usually don't see that we add our own needs and desires to the situations we come in contact with. We don't see how impermanent and interrelated everything is.

When we look deeply and practice mindfulness in our businesses we can see the essence of our business, what is unique about our particular offering and also what is not unique. We can see the cycle of our business from its inception to its demise. We can also see more clearly what steps we need to take to grow and how to pull back when necessary. With mindfulness we can feel our true happiness and help others to be happy. We can take actions that relieve our suffering and the suffering of others, foster letting go of habits that do not help us, and help us to become freer and more authentic. As a result we can be more effective in the way we work with others and in guiding our business toward meeting our customers' needs.

You might experiment with some regular mindfulness exercises at work. When the telephone rings, use this as an opportunity to take a breath. Know that there is someone on the other end of the line also breathing. Each time you turn your computer on or off, stop and take a deep breath. While sitting at your desk, notice how your body feels — the sensation of your feet touching the floor, the feeling of your back against your chair. Try relaxing your shoulders and your neck.

QUESTIONS FOR DAILY PRACTICE

- Ask yourself, Who is it that is breathing?

- Do you have to do anything for breathing to happen?

- How does paying attention to your breathing affect your understanding?

- What sensations arise in your body as you're sitting, talking, walking?

IT'S WHAT YOU SAY:
RIGHT SPEECH

There is a Zen story about two groups of monks arguing over a cat. The teacher, in response to the conflict, picks up the cat in one hand and a knife in the other. He says to the group of monks, "Say something of the truth of Zen, or I will cut the cat in half." No one said anything, and the cat was killed. (Remember, this is a story — I've always imagined that the teacher pretended to kill the cat.) Later, the teacher was describing this event to one of his most revered students. Upon hearing what had happened, this student, without saying a word, took off his sandals, put them on his head, and left the room. The teacher said, "If only you had been there, the cat would have been saved."

What did this student do to save the cat? What does this story have to do with business and our work lives?

Several months ago I was in a staff meeting in which I was feeling uncomfortable. We were discussing our product-development strategy for the next six months. I felt that there were conflicts and unresolved issues among my managers and staff. We were not all in agreement and were not all working together. My attempts at achieving clarity and a unified vision did not seem to be working as well as I would have liked. In the midst of this meeting, I felt an opening, a chance to guide the discussion and at the same time to transform our strategies. Being preoccupied with trying to say the right thing, I hesitated. I was concerned about making a mistake. The discussion progressed. The time no longer seemed right to make my point. I had missed my chance to say something that could make a difference. I had "killed the cat."

In the story above the student would have saved the cat by fully meeting the teacher. He didn't hesitate. He responded to another person in a way that was direct and authentic. He wasn't trying to look good, wasn't trying to think of a clever or even a clear answer. He acted. He wasn't caught by his past and wasn't thrown off center by his teacher. He responded, without using words.

One of the amazing aspects of business is the way in which we all bring our communication styles, often including our childhood habits, and strengths and weaknesses into the workplace. Businesses often spend a good deal of time creating systems in an attempt to root out or change these individual behaviors, but we are all human beings with established ways of communicating and responding. We often underestimate the power that our words have.

The definition of right speech is to speak truthfully, being loyal to the truth when speaking with others, not creating harm or speaking cruelly, not exaggerating or embellishing, and speaking in a way that relieves suffering and brings people back to themselves. Let's discuss these aspects in more detail.

BEING LOYAL TO THE TRUTH

Saying what you know to be true and not saying what is not true is a clear and powerful practice — and much more difficult than you might imagine. When we speak truthfully we become worthy of trust, and the people around us feel cared for and safe.

In my business, most of our customers buy directly from us and have thirty days to pay for their purchase. If they are late paying us, we call them. I think of this as an opportunity for truth telling. Our policy regarding collections calls is merely to state the truth — reminding customers of what they purchased, when they purchased it, the amount they owe, and when the payment was due. We then ask them when they expect to make a payment. In return for stating the truth we ask for the truth in return.

Of course, we also make our purchases on credit. It can be more difficult being on the other end of these calls, but the practice is the same. If we are late in making payments, we try to call our vendors before we are called. We let them know we are aware of the payment due and relate our plan for making the payment, especially if we will be late. Sometimes just telling the truth can be very refreshing, even though it can also be painful.

NOT CREATING HARM

Our words have the power to cause tremendous harm or tremendous healing. I've seen much pain caused in the work environment by people not being careful with speech and underestimating the power of words. Even when we have no intention to cause harm, our words may affect our colleagues in ways that are completely outside our own experience or expectations. I have noticed, as a manager and especially as "the boss," that my words, particularly how I express my displeasure, can have a tremendous impact. I have learned the importance of giving great care to where, when, and how I express my insights regarding performance or behaviors that need to be changed or improved.

NOT EXAGGERATING

So often in business, people describe situations and outcomes in ways that make themselves or their projects appear more successful or more certain than they really are. I have also noticed that people sometimes make tasks appear more difficult and complicated than they actually are as a way to protect themselves from criticism or from being given additional work. The word *spin*, meaning to put a positive — or negative — light on a situation, has recently been in vogue. Spin is just a euphemism for exaggeration.

Some years ago I noticed that in my communication with the Brush Dance board of directors I was presenting information in a very positive way and underestimating what was not working well. When I realized this, my first reaction was to overcompensate. For a while I was underemphasizing our successes and bringing lots of attention to the difficulties. Now I try to present the most accurate picture that I can of our successes, our failures, what I'm feeling good about, and my concerns.

RELIEVING SUFFERING

Our speech has the potential to provide comfort, positive challenge, and transformation in our work environment. By speaking clearly and directly from our hearts, we can touch the people around us and turn suffering into acceptance and joy. Just listening fully to others is often enough to relieve suffering. This requires stopping and just being with another person, in whatever state they are in.

I was recently surprised to discover that aspects of my management style and speech were habits I had learned as a child. When I was very young I sensed the tension and stress in my household. My father was manic-depressive and in and out of mental institutions. There was very little talk in my household about feelings, difficulties, or needs. I developed a strategy of dealing with difficult situations by ignoring them or distancing myself from them. Things seemed difficult enough, in fact teetering on the edge of disaster. I concluded that if I were to express what I saw or needed, it might push the situation over the edge or make it worse. I learned not to say anything about the painful situation at hand and just take care of myself and of my parents the best I could.

Though this strategy may have worked for me as a child, it could have proved disastrous for me as the CEO of a small, quickly growing company. Not saying anything was seen by some as approval of their behavior and work performance and by others as an expression of disapproval. Of course, usually it was the employees who were acting inappropriately and not performing well who thought my silence meant that I approved of their work, and the employees who were excelling who felt unacknowledged by my silence.

The foundation of right speech is deep listening. Our speech does not occur in a vacuum — it must include our awareness of others. When people don't feel heard they become isolated and unhappy. Their work suffers, and the work of everyone around them suffers as well. Right speech means being present and meeting each person and each situation directly. Since each person has different communication and listening styles, right speech is the practice of speaking to each person in a way that best reaches and affects that person in each situation, while at the same time being true to yourself.

Sometimes we can use speech to hide our feelings and intentions.

We often do this by asking questions instead of just saying what we want, see, or feel. Other times we block out others' viewpoints by not asking questions and by forcefully entering others' space. Practicing right speech entails including many views and expressing information and feeling in a way that is clear, direct, and effective.

Notice how you speak to others and how others speak to you. Just notice. Notice how your speech varies with whomever you are speaking to — someone whom you report to, who reports to you, a family member. Try speaking directly and openly. Take risks with your words by speaking openly from your heart. Notice how your words touch and affect people. Experiment with beginning your sentences with the words "I want," "I need," and "I feel." Make statements instead of asking questions. Use your speech to be clear, open, direct, and vulnerable.

QUESTIONS FOR DAILY PRACTICE

- What does right speech mean to you?

- What is not right speech?

- Can you just listen, or are you formulating a response?

- How can saying nothing be right speech?

- In what situations do you exaggerate?

- Have experiences from your childhood or other work situations influenced how you speak now in work situations? Which of these experiences are useful, and which get in your way?

- How does your speech affect your feelings and your energy?

IT'S WHAT YOU DO:
RIGHT ACTION

One of my most difficult business decisions was letting go of twelve people in one day. This was at a time when Brush Dance was pursuing an Internet strategy. In just a few months we had grown from ten to twenty-two employees. Then, six months later, as the environment for Internet businesses plunged, our investment group announced that they had decided to stop funding the Internet business. We had completely run out of money and needed to take some dramatic steps to save the wholesale business. There appeared to be no choice but to let go of our employees who were working primarily on the Internet side of the business and to cut back on the number of people working for the wholesale division.

Letting go of people who had worked hard for the company, in some cases for many years, in a way that felt true, authentic, and compassionate was painful and challenging. I met individually with most of the employees who were being let go. I explained the history of our growth, the circumstances that had led to the current situation, and our thinking about the steps we needed to take to save the company. I shared my pain and my vulnerability. Many of these meetings were difficult and heartfelt, often filled with tears. In the midst of the pain and difficulty of these encounters, there was real human connection. I learned that sometimes just one word or a smile can help transform someone's difficulty.

Right action can be defined simply as doing good and avoiding harm. Right action is intimately connected to right view, right thinking, and right speech. Our views, thinking, and speech cannot be separated from how we act. I once heard a teacher explain that the essence of Zen is just to "not make things worse," highlighting just how difficult it is to be a human being. Zen defines doing good as expressing compassion, cultivating kindness, working toward ending social injustice, and being generous with your time and energy.

Compassion. Zen defines compassion as acting to relieve and transform difficulty. In business we often have the opportunity to practice compassion with people with whom we come into contact. This might include colleagues who are just beginning a new job or who for whatever reason are leaving the workplace. Sometimes just fully listening to others' difficulties, whether work related or not, can be an act of compassion.

Kindness. We may not think of our jobs as a place to practice kindness, but why not? We are all vulnerable human beings, even at work, or especially at work. The more we recognize and acknowledge this truth, the more we can be ourselves, and the better we can perform. I find kindness to be one of the most valuable practices in the workplace.

Social justice. Nearly every business has the opportunity to work toward social justice, internally or externally, directly or indirectly. Does your company practice social justice in its hiring practices and in compensation, roles, and responsibilities? Does your company have policies and standards in working with your vendors and customers that foster fairness and equality? How can you bring about fairness and justice within your company and in relationship to your community?

Generosity. Work provides constant opportunities to practice generosity. Our time and our energy are precious gifts that we can choose to withhold or choose to give freely. A student asked his teacher, "I am discouraged, what should I do?" The teacher responded, "Encourage others." Being generous, most fundamentally, is seeing that we are all intimately, deeply connected. Helping ourselves is helping others; helping others is helping ourselves. We don't help others for our own benefit or to get something. We see that someone needs us, and we make ourselves available.

Right action is paying attention. How do you act when you feel uncomfortable or threatened? What pushes your buttons? In what situation do you feel uncomfortable? The more we pay attention, the more we learn about ourselves. The more we pay attention to our actions, we see how difficult it is to consistently act in a way that is aligned with our values and intentions. It is said that the life of a Zen teacher can be defined as "one mistake following another."

Several years ago Brush Dance decided to produce T-shirts. We wanted to take our best-selling card designs and put them onto organic, unbleached cotton shirts. We decided to offer both organic cotton and regular white cotton shirts, at the smallest price differential possible. Though this carried some financial risks, we believed that it could potentially bring us both financial and environmental gains as well. We believed that this was the right action to take. We were surprised and disappointed to see the results — store buyers ordered many more of the bleached shirts than the organic cotton shirts. Though this campaign was not as successful as planned, we learned that though we sold many more white shirts, we were able to introduce many buyers to the advantages of organic cotton.

Right action is the practice of coming into contact with our caring, love, and vulnerability. It is the practice of seeing and acting strategically by understanding that there is no conflict, no difference, between taking care of ourselves, taking care of the people we work with, and taking care of the mission and goals of our organization.

Notice what you do when you first come to work. Notice what you do as you are preparing to leave work. Notice how your thinking and speech affect what you do and how what you do affects your thinking and your speech.

QUESTIONS FOR DAILY PRACTICE

- What are your most basic patterns and habits?

- Do these give you energy or drain your energy?

- What kinds of actions at work lead you to feeling good or not feeling good?

- When are you acting out of habit?

- When are you acting to help others?

- What actions bring you toward joy and freedom?

- What actions increase your pain?

- Who controls your actions?

- What routines and patterns can you add to your daily life that would be nurturing and satisfying, settling and conducive to your well-being?

IT'S YOUR WORK:
RIGHT LIVELIHOOD

Brush Dance began in 1989 as an environmental products mail-order catalog. Our first product was wrapping paper made from recycled paper. We were one of the first companies in the United States to produce wrapping paper that was made from more than 50 percent recycled paper, including 10 percent post-consumer waste. Our first designs were created when I proposed the idea of making environmentally friendly wrapping paper to Mayumi Oda, an internationally known artist. Mayumi loved the idea and appeared at my home a few days later with several extraordinary designs.

The first time that wrapping paper was delivered to the company I gained insight into some of the complexities regarding right livelihood. At this time Brush Dance was operating from my house, as it did for the first three years of its history. A truck pulled up to my home, and we unloaded thirty boxes of wrapping paper. My heart sank. I looked at this paper and thought, "Is this really right livelihood? Do people really need wrapping paper? It certainly doesn't seem like a necessity." I thought that the world might be better off without it at all. And even though the paper was made from recycled paper, trees were still being used to make it. The truck that delivered it was burning oil to bring it to us. At that moment I realized just how complicated this issue of right livelihood can be.

The classic definition of right livelihood in Buddhism is work that does not include dealing in arms, slave trade, the meat industry, the arms industry, or in predicting the future. From the perspective of our complex, interconnected lives, if we eat meat or dairy products, we are connected to the meat industry. If we pay taxes to a government that makes weapons, we have a relationship with the arms industry. If we look closely, nearly every American spends a good portion of their work time working for the government. I am not proposing that everyone stop drinking milk and stop paying taxes. My point is for us to be aware and to understand the complexity of our lives. My hope is that paying attention will foster humility, insight, and action.

Through your actions, through the way you respond, you can change the world. Your livelihood, the work you choose and the way you do it, can be healing and transformative — for yourself, for the people you work with, for our society, and for our planet. Business may be the most powerful and influential force on our planet. You can choose to work for positive change by responding to what is needed, and you can act in a way that continues to do harm.

It can be easy to judge ourselves and others in regard to right livelihood. We live in complex, difficult times where everything is interconnected. We talk on phones that are made in faraway lands, in factories and by people who would be nearly impossible to trace. Our cars use oil that comes from many parts of the world. Our food is often the source of tremendous suffering, causing erosion and degrading of the environment, usually far removed from our daily experience.

It is possible to work for an arms manufacturer and be of tremendous benefit to the people around you. It is possible to work for a hospice or homeless shelter and cause harm or stress through your actions and habits. Right livelihood is the practice of questioning, uncovering, not settling for what is easy or on the surface. Ask yourself, Is my work benefiting others, or is it causing harm? Is the way I think, speak, and act at work benefiting or causing harm?

At the base of Zen practice is what are referred to as the Three Pure Precepts:

1. Do good.

2. Avoid doing harm.

3. Help others.

Right livelihood is *making the effort* to do good, avoiding doing harm, and helping others in the kind of work we do, in the results and effects of our work, in the conditions of our workplace, and in how we interact with our colleagues. It is important to recognize that this effort, this practice, is complex, difficult, and impossible. And yet we also recognize that we have no choice but to make our best effort, moment after moment.

QUESTIONS FOR DAILY PRACTICE

- What are some of your attitudes and actions at work that help or hinder other people?

- What are some ways in which the work you do benefits others?

- What is your vision of expressing right livelihood?

- What is your plan for cultivating this vision?

- What stops you from living this vision now?

- What about your work is right livelihood?

- What about your work is not right livelihood?

- What changes can you make to move your work toward right livelihood?

STAYING WITH IT:
RIGHT DILIGENCE

While searching for a job in New York after I received my MBA, I changed my résumé each time I failed to find a job. I've sometimes thought that I could put a book together showing how my résumé evolved to make my previous work experiences appear more understandable! I learned the importance of telling my story so that it addressed the specific needs of prospective employers. I learned that a résumé is both a record of previous accomplishments and a statement of potential. Still, the fact that I had been a Zen student for many years did not appear to open doors. My position as Director of Tassajara, Zen Mountain Center, changed on my résumé to become Human Resources Director of Tassajara, a California resort.

I interviewed for several months, determined to get a job as a trainer in the New York corporate world. I went on numerous interviews and made several presentations. I had some talented mentors who taught me how to dress (including the importance of wearing the right socks, belt, and necktie), how to tell my story, and how to conduct myself in a job interview. After several months and many meetings I was getting discouraged. One day the woman interviewing me at a small consulting company read my résumé and said, "Who are you kidding? I'm familiar with Tassajara. It's a monastery!" I had no idea what to think of her discovery. She smiled, and we connected. She said she trusted me because of my Zen background, and I was hired for my first business management job in New York City. My persistence had paid off, albeit in an unusual way!

Diligence means making constant, careful, and steady effort. In the context of work, and our lives, the key issue is the aim of our steady effort. From the usual perspective, at work our goal is to maximize profits for our own benefit, to increase our material value, and to have as much control, power, and predictability as possible. From the perspective of Zen, our effort is toward freedom, flexibility, happiness, compassion, and social justice. Profits, power, and control can be used toward these goals, but they are not ends in themselves.

Our work lives are transformed when we practice diligence — using each moment and each situation to move away from habits and patterns that cause pain and toward building character and developing a flexible, open mind. In forging our paths we have no choice but to start where we are. We have no choice but to move ahead, not knowing what will happen.

Right diligence means not getting thrown off our path. We notice, over and over, when we have not lived up to our expectations, and we try again. After I left the Zen Center community to pursue my MBA I lived in Great Neck, New York. Somehow I met one of the few, and perhaps only, other Buddhist practitioners in Great Neck. Brenda and I started a small meditation group in her living room, and we sat meditation together several mornings a week. We did this for several months and then noticed that several months would go by without our sitting together. We would speak to each other and begin again, sitting regularly for many months. This pattern repeated itself three or four times. One day we were discussing what to name our little meditation group, and we decided on "Let's try it again," hanging a sign with those very words.

The effort and path of integrating Zen practice and work require tremendous diligence. Just trying to practice Zen is impossible. Just trying to make a living is impossible. Who would be foolish enough to try to combine the two?

QUESTIONS FOR DAILY PRACTICE

- What kinds of work activities do you find discouraging?

- What kinds of work activities do you find invigorating and renewing?

- What do you do when you want to give up? What are your options?

- When have you felt that you did not stay with something long enough?

- When did you stay too long in a particular place, job, or relationship?

STAYING FOCUSED:
RIGHT CONCENTRATION

I was captain of my high school wrestling team during my senior year of Colonia High School in New Jersey. One of the
teams we faced was J. P. Stevens High School from Edison. They
were consistently one of the top-rated teams in the state and regularly sent wrestlers to the state championship. During the warm-up
period, my team behaved like most wrestling teams. We ran briskly
onto the mats, did some exercises, and made a lot of noise. The
main objective of our warm-up was to demonstrate our prowess to
the opposing team.

In contrast, the J. P. Stevens team walked out slowly and quietly onto the wrestling mat. They were poised, focused, and con-
centrated, preparing themselves for the task ahead by settling and
quieting their minds. They seemed uninterested in our team. Their
uniforms were black, and their heads were nearly shaved. They
didn't talk or smile. I knew right away that this was the team I
wanted to be on. I think of this as an early sign of my desire to be
a Zen monk.

One of the things that intrigued me in high school wrestling
was the power, passion, and complexity of concentration. I noticed
that my desire to win and my fear of losing often interfered with

my performance, my concentration, and my enjoyment. I knew that something very important was going on, and I also felt that something very vital was missing. By my senior year I was a fairly good wrestler, having faced some of the better competition in the state. Competing with the best in the state was, as my coach proclaimed, a good way to develop. Our coach used to ask, "Do you want to be a big fish in a small pond, or a big fish in a large pond?" This was his way of explaining that although we were a new and inexperienced team, it was useful to wrestle against the best teams in the state, even if it meant being utterly demolished and embarrassed.

In watching other wrestlers I noticed that the good ones were usually strong and athletic and really wanted to win. The best wrestlers, those who became state champions, seemed different. They weren't always the strongest or quickest or the most athletic looking. They certainly cared about winning, but they did not seem caught up in winning and losing. Rather, they appeared focused on what they were doing. They seemed to move and act from a deeper place than the good wrestlers. They often seemed a little odd and appeared not to care what others thought of them. I knew that there was something to learn from these wrestlers and that the lessons to be learned would translate far beyond the wrestling mat.

I notice now that the people I most admire in business have similar qualities to the wrestlers who were the state champions — they are not the smartest or most aggressive people. Successful businesspeople often seem quiet and sometimes shy. (Of course, there are many exceptions to this!) They appear somewhat unusual. They seem to be having fun and at the same time are present and aware. I notice a quality in them that I would describe as *concentration*.

Zen practice describes two kinds of concentration, active and selective, that can be applied to our work lives. Active concentration is similar to mindfulness; it is focusing on whatever is arising in the moment. We appreciate and pay attention to whatever comes along. We are not judging or evaluating but just listening to what is being said, just seeing what is right in front of us.

Selective concentration is choosing a particular object or practice. We can use concentration to solve a quantitative problem or to design a new marketing campaign. Developing and using concentration can transform the way we perform a host of activities in our work lives. Three traditional objects of concentration can be applied to our work lives: concentration on impermanence, concentration on interrelatedness, and concentration on nonself. Let's take a look at these now.

IMPERMANENCE

The Buddha suggested that one way to grasp impermanence is to picture our body after we have died. This practice involves seeing our body decaying, being eaten by insects, turning from the familiar human form to bones, then dust, and then returning to the Earth. Similarly, I suggest that you concentrate on the work you are doing as no longer existing. Concentrate on the fact that the company you work for will someday not exist. Imagine your work space as no longer being your work space. Picture it as a forest or an empty field.

By acknowledging and experiencing the fleeting nature of your life, your awareness can drop down to a deeper place, where what really matters comes more clearly into focus and your appreciation for your workplace that does exist can heighten.

INTERRELATEDNESS

Concentration on the interrelatedness of all things is critical in working with people and in evaluating and implementing our business strategy. How we interact with each person we work with affects the entire team and the efforts of the company. How we organize or participate in a meeting affects the daily atmosphere, future meetings, and the success of the company.

In discussing interrelatedness Thich Nhat Hanh says, "If you are a poet you will see clearly that there is a cloud floating in this sheet of paper. Without a cloud there will be no rain, the trees cannot grow; and without trees we cannot make paper. The cloud is essential for the paper to exist. If the cloud is not here the sheet of paper cannot be here either. So we can say that the cloud and the paper inter-are."

It is striking for me to realize that I have never done anything in business by myself. The name of the business was inspired by one of my teachers. The capital used to start the business came from family and friends. I need the skills of others who know about computers, software, phone systems, legal issues, and accounting issues. The business requires customers and vendors and artists. Every aspect of our work lives is completely interdependent.

NONSELF

Concentration on nonself means not being attached to the images and ideas we have about ourselves. Practicing nonself is not taking things personally. Success or failure is not something that "I" did. We make our best effort in each moment, without being caught up in the illusion of what "I" accomplished, or didn't accomplish, separate from all the interactions we have with others.

A golf study I read describes filming the swings of beginning and intermediate golfers and comparing their swings to those of professional golfers. These golfers were filmed hitting a golf ball and then filmed when they were just swinging, with no ball to hit. In nearly every case, the swings of beginning golfers look more like the swings of professional golfers when they are swinging without trying to hit a ball. The conclusion from this study is that effort, trying for a result, gets in the way of the natural wisdom and knowledge contained in our bodies. Sometimes effort, our trying for a particular result, gets in the way.

QUESTIONS FOR DAILY PRACTICE

- How have others contributed to your work life?

- If you could be at your own funeral, who would be there? What are people saying about you?

- Who is this "I" that you call yourself at work? Is this the same "I" or a different "I" from the "I" at home?

- Is there anything permanent about your work — the people, the place, the products?

- How have others contributed to your work?

- How have you came to do the work you do?

WISDOM:
YOUR ORDINARY MIND
IS THE PATH

GENEROSITY

Ten minutes. That was the amount of time allowed to make a presentation to a group of one hundred and fifty prospective investors. I had been invited, along with fifteen other company founders, to a conference of socially responsible investors being held in Southern California. I had ten minutes to capture their attention, to describe Brush Dance's history, strategies, and plans for the future, and to make a compelling case for the financial and social benefits of investing money in Brush Dance at this time. These investors were using two criteria in making their decisions: 1) Was this a good financial investment? What was the likelihood that the company would meet its goals and that the investment would reap a solid return? 2) Was this company meeting some kind of social or environmental need and not causing social or environmental harm?

After each company's presentations were made, the group of investors met privately in a large conference room to discuss the strengths and weaknesses of each business and to share information. I found out after the conference that someone I barely knew, a man named Peter, stood up in front of this group as they were discussing each business and said, "We need to provide money to

Brush Dance. Marc is a really good guy, and this is a worthwhile business to invest in." I was moved by Peter's generosity when I heard this from one of the investors who had attended the meeting. It is one of those extraordinary, anonymous acts that has stayed with me as an example of generosity.

Everything we think of as ours, our bodies and minds and all the material things that make up our lives, has been given to us. The air we breathe and the water we drink are gifts. Everything we do in our work has been taught to us or given to us by someone else. All work, all business, is centered around giving — we give food, goods, services, and comfort.

Zen offers several different views and practices regarding generosity. Thich Nhat Hanh says, "The greatest gift we can offer is our presence." He goes on to explain that we can also offer our stability, our freedom, our happiness, our freshness, and our peace.

Presence. Just being present to those we work with, just listening fully as a human being, is perhaps the greatest gift we can offer at work. So often we are caught up in our tasks and our busyness. Just stopping and being present can transform our environment and open us in unexpected ways.

Stability. We offer our stability by bringing a calm and clear mind to our work. We offer stability by staying out of the dramas, by not taking sides, by not wobbling. We offer our stability by just being ourselves, moment after moment.

Freedom. Offering our freedom is encouraging others by acting from our own independence, our own ability to make choices. We offer freedom by not being afraid to speak and act for what we deeply believe.

Happiness. Allowing ourselves to feel happy at work can be a tremendous act of generosity to ourselves and to those around us.

Our own happiness is perhaps our dearest birthright, not to be ignored or sacrificed at work.

Freshness. Imagine coming to work, fresh and renewed, as if it were a new day, like no other day. Isn't this a fact?

Peace. Our workplace is where peace can begin. Peace is not something that just happens but a moment-to-moment act, a practice of generosity.

Dogen said, "When we understand completely, being born and dying are both forms of giving. All productive labor is fundamentally giving. Giving is to transform the mind of living beings. One should not calculate the greatness or smallness of the mind, nor the greatness or smallness of the thing. Nevertheless, there is a time when the mind transforms things, and there is giving in which things transform the mind."

How often in our work lives are we so focused on tasks that we forget the importance of being present to our colleagues? At work we have many opportunities to be generous with our time, knowledge, and understanding. We can give others our trust and confidence.

The practice of generosity is giving ourselves over to what we are doing. The first step in Zen practice is to start where you are, to fully accept your strengths and weaknesses, your talents and your limitations. This is an act of generosity with yourself. Generosity is a vital ingredient in moving toward doing good and avoiding harm.

Decide to perform an act of generosity each week. Do something generous that is anonymous, without feeling pride. Just do it. (A friend of mine regularly pays the toll for the car behind him when he pays the toll at a tollbooth). Choose an act of generosity to practice — presence, stability, freedom, and so forth. Write it down. Notice what draws you to this practice as well as what hinders you from it. Notice how others practice or don't practice generosity in your workplace.

QUESTIONS FOR DAILY PRACTICE

- How do you practice generosity at work? ·

- What prevents you from being generous at work?

- Notice how it feels to give and to receive. What does it feel like when you give someone your money, your time, or your praise? What does it feel like to receive money or someone else's time or praise?

- Are you more comfortable giving or receiving?

- What parts of giving and receiving feel like hindrances? What opens you?

- Who is your model at work for practicing generosity?

ETHICAL CONDUCT

My wife recently asked me to give her the names of some graphic designers and to describe their particular capabilities. I wrote her an email, describing the two designers we use and outlined what I felt were their strengths and their limitations. I mistakenly sent this email to the designers instead of to my wife. I received a phone message from one of the designers, who was quite upset by having received my email, though I hadn't said anything particularly negative. While I was thinking about how I should respond to this situation I noticed that I started to feel more and more angry with my wife. I noticed that what was going through my mind was, "If only my wife had not asked me for the names of these designers, I would not have gotten into this mess." Fortunately, I was able to laugh at myself.

When we practice ethical conduct we acknowledge the reality that we live and work with other people. We all have the ability to cause harm. We all make choices. Our actions have consequences. Ethical conduct in Zen practice can be summarized in what are called the Three Pure Precepts: do good, avoid harm, help others. From the perspective of Zen practice, ethical conduct is both a guideline for and expression of an awakened mind. Ethical conduct is a way of describing awakened activity rather than a list of hard-and-fast rules. Instead, the precepts provide guidelines and a path toward realizing our own natures and toward opening our hearts.

Zen also describes what are called the Ten Grave Precepts. Each of these can be applied to our work lives:

Not killing. This precept might include not killing time and not killing opportunities to help others. It also might include the necessity of working for peace.

Not taking what is not given. This precept includes not taking from others, not taking money, not making personal long-distance phone calls during work, and not taking others' ideas.

Not misusing sex. This precept includes not being completely honest and open to real intimacy.

Not speaking falsely. This precept says to speak the truth, to speak honestly, not to lie, and to speak from your heart.

Not giving or taking drugs. This precept says to trust in your mind just as it is, without taking any mind-changing drugs.

Not discussing the faults of others. This precept is very important in work settings. It requires not speaking about other people and not triangulating, saying things to someone about a third person that you have not said directly to that person.

Not praising self at the expense of others. This precept advises us not to put others down and to speak in a way that is respectful and that makes others feel their worth.

Not being selfish. The precept advises us not to act from a place of tightness but instead to act from a sense of abundance and with an open heart.

Not indulging in anger. Although expressing anger can be healthy and useful, this precept tells us that indulging in anger creates harm and disharmony.

Not living a life not based in practice. This precept underlines the need to frame all activities within the context of practice: doing good, avoiding harm, helping others.

The issue of ethical conduct has become more and more relevant in business and work during the past few years. Business leaders who lie and steal or do not adhere to ethical conduct are capable of causing tremendous and long-lasting harm to many people. Ethical conduct in many ways is the backbone for living and working within a life of practice.

In an often-told Zen story, a student once asked, "Is a completely awakened person free from cause and effect?" The teacher answered, "Yes, a completely awakened person is free from cause and effect." Because of this answer the teacher is turned into a fox for five hundred lifetimes. This story was told to demonstrate that no one is free of the consequences of their actions.

QUESTIONS FOR DAILY PRACTICE

- Which of the Ten Grave Precepts do you find most relevant to your work life? In what ways?

- How do you practice ethical conduct at work?

- In what ways is the practice of ethical conduct most challenging for you?

- Which of the precepts is the most difficult for you?

PATIENCE

I have now been the CEO of Brush Dance for more than fifteen years. When I look back at the initial business plan that I wrote in 1989 I see that we have achieved exactly what I set out to achieve in terms of revenues, product line, and distribution. It took us fifteen years instead of the projected three years to reach these benchmarks. I sometimes describe Brush Dance as an overnight success — that took fifteen years to achieve.

I also did not project the ups and downs, the near-bankruptcies, the comings and goings of employees. I never expected the pain of wondering how we were going to meet payroll and the worry about how to keep the business going when the financial picture looked completely bleak. I had no idea that we would transform into an Internet company, that my board would hire (and then fire) a CEO to manage the company, and that it would take years to transform the company back into being a wholesale business.

I sometimes think that Zen students and entrepreneurs are the most patient, and at the same time the least patient, people. Zen students spend long hours, days, and years, sitting, facing a wall, expecting nothing. Entrepreneurs spend a tremendous amount of time, energy, and money planning and working without knowing the results of their efforts. While Zen students and entrepreneurs exhibit great patience they are equally impatient when it comes to accepting anything less than perfection.

Basho, a Zen poet wrote:

Fleas, lice
The horse pissing
Near my pillow

This poem describes the rawness of Basho's life and his ability to describe things just the way they are. My poem for today could be something like:

Email not working
Employees out sick
Little accomplished

Our lives at work are filled with difficulty. People are late for meetings. Our ideas are not met with enthusiasm. Computers crash, restart, and crash again. Other people don't meet our expectations. Our overnight package is lost. Relationships become impossible. Cash shortages are threatening, and businesses fail. Patience requires that we fully and directly face our difficulties, that we embrace and learn from situations and from our feelings about them. Owning and transforming our pain and disappointment can be a tremendous challenge, as well as a tremendous gift.

Patience is what connects the entrepreneurial spirit required in business with facing the truth of what is actually required in Zen practice. It takes patience to face the truth of where we are in our work lives. The truth may include the pain of not meeting expectations, a variety of messy and challenging situations facing us each day, as well as the possibilities of transformation and great accomplishment.

Zen describes several kinds of patience that can be practiced at work: acceptance of difficulty and hardship, not acting hastily, and acceptance of what is true. Let's explore these.

Acceptance of difficulty. Our lives at work can be transformed when we completely accept that difficulty is to be expected and cannot be avoided. This doesn't mean we take the negative attitude of "what will go wrong today?" Instead, we just pay attention to our own state of mind. We make our best effort. We meet each situation as it arises.

Not acting hastily. Given how difficult, unpredictable, and stressful our work lives can be, it is easy to respond quickly and impatiently. In difficult situations, just stop, think, and look more carefully at what really is the cause of the difficulty. When your computer crashes you can get upset and yell at whoever is in charge of your computer systems. Or, when your computer crashes, what if you just stop, take a breath, and notice your breathing, notice what is around you?

Acceptance of what is true. Most of our impatience comes from our wanting things to be different from what they are. Our overnight package did not arrive overnight. This is just true. There is nothing we can do to change what is. We can take actions to expedite the package's delivery, but this action includes accepting what is difficult, not acting hastily, and accepting what is true.

QUESTIONS FOR DAILY PRACTICE

- Notice when you are patient and when you are impatient at work.

- Write down and fill in — I feel patient when... It is hard for me to feel patient when...

- Notice what is most difficult for you at work. What part of this difficulty do you create? How can you transform this difficulty?

- How do your thinking and your speech affect your patience?

- How does your patience level affect your thinking and your speech?

- What pushes your buttons?

- What events cause you to get angry?

- How do you view and respond to anger?

ENERGY AND ZEAL

Right now my life is just one learning experience after another.... By the end of the week I should be a genius.

When I was a full-time student at New York University's Graduate School of Business, I commuted to school five days a week, one and a half hours each way — a half-hour walk to the train station, a half-hour train ride to Manhattan, and a half hour on the subway. I also worked twenty hours a week for a management consulting company, and I spent four to eight hours every day taking care of our infant son while my wife worked or went to graduate school. I read and studied early in the mornings or late at night. I sat meditation each morning and also began a newsletter called *From the Marketplace,* pulling together stories from friends who had left the San Francisco Zen Center and were engaged in the world outside the center. I was highly motivated in my quest to learn about business and to integrate my Zen experience with the business world.

Now, as CEO of Brush Dance, I'm constantly stretched to find the energy it takes to transform myself and the company. My life very much feels like "rocks in a tumbler": hard boulders hitting each other, again and again, constantly becoming smoother and smoother, the edges being worn down. Each day I bump into my own habits and patterns, my own deepest pain and longing, as well as the habits, patterns, and pain of those working around me. I strive for clarity and sometimes create confusion. The life of a Zen student or teacher and the life of a businessperson or leader can be described as "one mistake following another." Staying with it and staying focused on outer and inner transformation require tremendous energy.

Zen practice is often thought of as easygoing and contemplative. Spiritual practice, particularly Zen, requires tremendous energy, focus, and effort. There is an expression in Zen encouraging students to "practice as though your head were on fire." Looking inward, recognizing our habits and patterns, and then having the skill and courage to transform them is a deep, visceral process. Looking outward, working to transform the confusion, pain, and suffering in the workplace and in the world takes energy and focus.

Working with your head on fire means to work with intensity. Working with intensity does not mean that we act quickly or that we be in a rush. The combination of focus and intensity can often expand or obliterate our usual concepts of time. Intensity is a combination of focus, resolve, energy, and tenacity — focusing on the issue and not being distracted; working with resolve and determination; using your full energy, sometimes pacing yourself and sometimes moving quickly, much like a long-distance runner; and working with tenacity to go after a solution despite the difficulties and roadblocks.

One of the points I often raise in Company Time Workshops (a series of weekend retreats that combine spirituality and business) is that not only is it useful to look at ways spiritual practice can inform business, but it is also important to look at ways that practices and values developed in business can benefit and inform spiritual practice. An important value that the world of business has to offer to the world of spiritual practice is working with energy and a sense of urgency. In business, success and failure matter. Meeting goals matters. Meeting deadlines and delivering when agreed matter. When something is urgent in business, everything else takes a backseat to the matter at hand. This kind of energy can help to keep communication and actions crisp and clear, cutting through confusion and entanglements, distinguishing what really matters from what doesn't.

In Zen temples a wooden mallet is used to hit a wooden block to announce when it is time for meditation. Written on the back of the wooden block are characters that say, "Life and death are the great matters. Don't waste time." None of us knows when we will die. Zen teachers sometimes describe our lives as like being in a boat on an ocean, floating out to sea, knowing that someday our boat will sink — but having no idea when this will happen. Since we don't know when we will die, we should make our best effort right now. There is no reason to hold back, nothing to wait for. This kind of realization and acknowledgment of the shortness of our lives can help to provide the kind of visceral energy required to transform our businesses or our lives.

Another method used in Zen to facilitate the practice of energy is to ask the question "What is my purpose?" Our actions, priorities, and focus flow from the answer to this question. What are we really doing with our lives? What is the real purpose of the work we are doing?

There's a story about a group of American Zen teachers meeting with His Holiness the Dalai Lama. One of the teachers spoke about the problem of not having any time to take a vacation. The Dalai Lama was puzzled, not understanding this term. His interpreter tried several different ways to translate. Finally, when the Dalai Lama understood, he let out a robust and impish laugh. He asked, "Do bodhisattvas get time off?" (A bodhisattva is someone who dedicates his or her life to helping others.) The Dalai Lama was commenting that there is no time off from using our energy to transform suffering into joy and to continually meet the needs of others.

I was a young student when Thich Nhat Hanh first visited Tassajara. He walked very slowly; all his movements seemed very measured. Someone once described Thich Nhat Hanh as a combination of a cat, a cloud, and a piece of heavy construction equipment. He was very calm, gentle, and at the same time very deliberate, intense, and filled with energy in his every action.

QUESTIONS FOR DAILY PRACTICE

- Try working at different paces. For half a day, work at a slow and steady pace. For another half day, try working with increased energy and intensity. Notice the difference.

- What activities give you energy? When do you feel most engaged?

- What activities drain your energy? When do you feel disengaged?

- What do you want to accomplish before you die?

- At your funeral, what accomplishments would you want noted in public?

MEDITATION:
LETTING GO OF EVERYTHING

Living at Tassajara, in the middle of a wilderness area, provided me with constant lessons in giving up ideas about what I thought was supposed to happen next. During my first winter in the valley, a week of winter rainstorms transformed the creek that flows through Tassajara into a raging river. As the water came close to overflowing its banks, I, along with the sixty residents, evacuated the meditation hall and quickly walked to higher ground. We stood together, wearing black meditation robes in the pouring rain, holding our open umbrellas, wondering if the meditation hall would be washed away. The following summer a huge forest fire surrounded Tassajara, and all the residents were forced to leave. I remember driving out on the dirt road, looking to the west, and seeing a tremendous wall of fire coming our way. That fall, the one-hundred-year-old meditation hall burned to the ground. A student had forgotten to blow out a lit kerosene lantern.

Meditation practice is the practice of letting go. It is the practice of sitting still, not going anywhere, being completely present to whatever arises. It is the practice of giving up the quest for fame and fortune, giving up your ordinary view of yourself and the need to be, think, or appear in any particular way. It is the practice of giving up assumptions about who we are and what we are supposed to be or do. Meditation is the practice of openheartedness, of complete and utter honesty, of purifying our character and developing integrity. It is the practice of compassion, of loving-kindness.

Seeing ourselves and the world as fresh is the starting point for integrating Zen practice and work practice. We ask ourselves, What is needed? How can I best respond to these needs? These are the questions, over and over, deeper and deeper, that we have to address in our work lives. Meditation practice provides the framework for opening ourselves to truly asking these questions and to being present for the answers.

One evening while I was preparing to fill a bathtub at Tassajara a bobcat entered the room and took the rubber stopper needed to fill the tub. I followed the bobcat as it walked away from the baths with the stopper in its mouth. I followed it as it walked up a hillside, trying to coax it to drop the stopper. As the bobcat sat down and began chewing on the stopper, I picked up a long broken branch from the ground, thinking I might use the stick to knock the stopper away from the bobcat. When the branch got near the bobcat, it put down the stopper, crouched on its hind legs, and began to move toward me. It was clear that this was the time to let go of my perceived need to get the stopper. This rubber stopper and my bath no longer seemed important in the context of life and death. I quickly backed away. No need for a bath this evening.

Meditation practice is recognizing the illusion that we can control what happens. When it floods, it floods. When buildings burn down, they burn down. Sometimes we face cash-flow shortages, we don't have enough sales, we find that our business has too much staff or not enough staff. Our challenge and our practice is to completely give ourselves to the situation at hand.

I was recently asked to give meditation instruction at the San Francisco Zen Center, where every Saturday morning people come from throughout the San Francisco Bay Area to 300 Page Street for guidance in starting a meditation practice. I had not given meditation instruction to a group like this for many years. I introduced myself and made eye contact with most of the thirty or so people looking at me. I laughed at myself when I realized that I had my cell phone, Palm Pilot, wallet, and keys in my pockets. I took out my cell phone, turned it off, and assured the group that these tools were not required for meditation practice.

This was a diverse group: people ranged in age from their early twenties to their sixties or seventies, a balance of men and women, from a variety of ethnic and economic backgrounds. Most appeared eager and open to learn how to meditate. Once everyone was gathered in the hallway near the front door, they followed me downstairs to the entranceway to the meditation hall. Everyone took off their shoes and awaited my instruction. I said that the first thing to do when entering the *zendo,* or meditation hall, is to bow toward the altar in the center of the room. Then I realized I needed to instruct them in the art of bowing.

Much of the practice of Zen is not casual. It is formal and contains many specific instructions. At the same time the practice is filled with heart and flexibility. The formality brings out a certain feeling of dignity. Everything is important; everything matters. The specificity creates a need to pay attention, to be mindful of your body, your movements, and your environment. Each is important.

"Put your hands together," I began, "palms touching palms, and fingers of each hand flat against each other. Your fingertips should be at about nose level and about a hand's-width distance from your nose. Your arms should be somewhat horizontal, elbows out, with some energy, not rigid and not limp. Then bow forward, from your waist, about thirty or forty-five degrees." I demonstrated and asked everyone to try it. Each person bowed. I noticed that every bow was completely different. Most were quite self-conscious. Some bowed quickly and others were slow; some a little tight or cautious.

I smiled as I watched them. Many people smiled in return. I said that the practice of bowing is much like the practice of meditation. Anyone can bow, anywhere and anytime. How can you "just bow" without anything extra, without trying to bow, without trying to do anything? I said that I thought it took a long time, perhaps years of practice, to just bow. To clarify, I talked a little about "beginner's mind": the simple state of being open, without preconceived ideas, doubts, hopes, or expectations. Just bowing doesn't mean making it into an absentminded routine or being self-conscious. "Just bow!"

"Notice what is extra in your bowing," I continued. "Notice when you are trying, holding, doing what is not necessary. Is there a way we want to be seen when we bow, or not seen? Are we hiding something or putting something forward? So much of our lives is like this: trying, doing what is extra and unnecessary, wanting to appear a certain way."

Perhaps by talking about bowing, I suggested, we had completed the essence of meditation instruction — a physical activity in which we practice just being with our bodies and our breath, with energy and attention, without doing anything extra. Then I proceeded to show them how to enter the zendo, to go to their seats, to sit down and get up, and how to leave the zendo. I told them to pay attention when in the zendo and follow the forms, and to not worry about the forms. "Watch, listen, be yourself, don't worry." Then we walked back upstairs for meditation instruction.

"Find a quiet, comfortable place to sit," I began again. "Sitting in a chair is fine, or sit on the floor using a pillow or meditation cushion. What is important is to sit, if possible, with your back straight and with some energy in your posture — shoulders slightly back, chin tucked in, your head pushing up slightly toward the ceiling, back slightly arched, your diaphragm pressed somewhat down and forward. You can put your hands on your knees or in the classic Zen mudra — left hand on top of your right, palms up, middle joints of your fingers meeting, and your thumbs slightly touching. The key is to sit in a way that is relaxed, comfortable, and with energy. Lean neither to the left nor the right.

"Keep your eyes open and look a few feet ahead of you without focusing on anything. Then, begin to pay attention to your body. Notice how your body feels. Notice where you are holding: is there any tightness in your shoulders, neck, or legs? Relax. Take a few deep breaths. Pay attention to your breathing. Let your breath come all the way in and all the way out, without your having to do anything. You can experiment with counting your exhales, from one to ten, and then begin again at one. If you lose count, as thinking or feelings arise, note what arises and begin again at one. Pay attention to your body, thoughts, and feelings. Keep coming back to your breathing.

"Make a schedule for yourself. Sitting early in the morning before daily activity begins may help you keep a schedule. Sit every morning or a few mornings a week. Join a sitting group, or find a partner or partners to sit with. Peer pressure and commitment help a lot in beginning the practice of meditation. Sit for ten or fifteen minutes, or thirty or forty minutes. Experiment and relax, with discipline and energy."

Another practice to experiment with during meditation is to

spend some time "turning," or focusing on, a question or a statement. Some questions that have arisen for me during the past year are: What is my life? What is most important to me? What can I contribute while here on this Earth? In your reading and exploring you may come across a story or poem that you want to incorporate into your sitting practice.

We had just a few minutes for questions before we needed to leave the room, where Saturday morning lecture would soon take place. A young woman asked, "What do I do when I feel angry during my meditation?" I suggested that she pay a lot of attention to her anger, to notice it, sit with it, and then return to her breathing, neither pushing the anger away or inviting it in.

I bowed and said thank you. They all bowed in return.

QUESTIONS FOR DAILY PRACTICE

- What is your meditation practice? What do you do? What is your experience?

- How is your meditation practice connected to your work?

- In what ways can you apply your meditation practice to your work life?

- In what ways is your meditation practice separate from your work life?

WISDOM:
YOUR ORDINARY MIND IS THE PATH

A student asked the teacher, "What is the true Zen path?" The teacher responded, "Your ordinary mind is the path."

The student said, "Should I try to direct myself toward it?"

The teacher replied, "If you try to direct yourself toward it, you will surely miss it."

The student asked, "How can I find the path if I don't direct myself toward it?"

The teacher responded, "Zen is not subject to knowing or not knowing. Knowing is delusion. Not knowing is worthless. When you are walking the Zen path your mind will be vast and boundless. How can this be a matter of finding or not finding?"

With these words the student was awakened.

What does it mean that "ordinary mind is the path?" How could this be? What does ordinary mind have to do with wisdom? What does wisdom have to do with work and with business?

If we think we are our work, this is not true. If we think we are separate from our work, this is also not true. We are our work, and we are separate from our work. This is the teaching of wisdom. Wisdom is experiencing the essential unity and connectedness of all things. Our body and mind are not two, and not one. Our body and mind are both two and one. We are neither independent nor dependent. At some point we will die. If we think this is the end of our life, this is not an accurate understanding. If we think we will not die, this is also not true.

When you view your work in terms of goals, achievements, money, and ambition, that is only one side. The other side, not to lose sight of, is uncovering your wisdom and the compassionate, sacred aspect of your work. But if you view your work only from the aspect of the sacred, you've left out the other side. Wisdom is embracing the sacred and the mundane, understanding that they are not different, not the same.

Brush Dance publishes a greeting card that says, "Wisdom is knowing what to do next." We also publish a greeting card known as the Irish Prayer. This card says,

> *Take time to work.*
> *It is the price of success.*
> *Take time to meditate.*
> *It is the source of power.*
> *Take time to play.*
> *It is the secret of perpetual youth.*
> *Take time to read.*
> *It is the way to knowledge.*
> *Take time to be friendly.*
> *It is the road to happiness.*
> *Take time to laugh.*
> *It is the music of the soul.*
> *And take time to love,*
> *And be loved.*

The Irish know a great deal about wisdom.

QUESTIONS FOR DAILY PRACTICE

- What is your definition of wisdom?

- What is your definition of ordinary mind?

- How do you think wisdom and ordinary mind are related?

- What place do wisdom and ordinary mind have in relation to work?

- How are the sacred and the mundane the same, and how are they different, from your work?

LISTENING TO YOUR
CLEAR, QUIET VOICE

RUN YOUR BUSINESS AND YOUR LIFE
LIKE A ZEN MONASTERY KITCHEN

My first week as head cook of Tassajara was exciting and challenging. I had completely underestimated how much food it took to feed one hundred and forty people three times a day. By my fourth day on the job we had almost completely run out of food. (Tassajara is two hours from the nearest food store.) I looked through the walk-in refrigerator, trying not to panic, and noticed that the only vegetable we had in any quantity was cabbage. Since there was not going to be another trip into town for two days, we found many creative ways to prepare cabbage — cabbage casserole, cabbage seaweed grill, and cabbage soup. I learned the importance of projecting inventory needs as well as making due with what was at hand, two skills that have served me well at Brush Dance.

I worked in the Tassajara kitchen for four summers and three winters. I was the dishwasher during my first summer, washing dishes by hand for three student meals and three guest meals each day. In the fall I worked on the kitchen crew, chopping vegetables and learning the basic skills of cooking and baking. The following summer I was the bread baker. Three years later, after I returned to Tassajara from Green Gulch Farm, I was the assistant cook for a summer and winter and then the head cook for a year.

The Tassajara kitchen is my model of the ideal environment for combining work practice and spiritual practice. Tassajara is a Zen monastery located deep in the mountains of central California, and it functions as a resort during the summer months. The kitchen often serves as the center of the monastery — the place where food is prepared and a place where work is most clearly an expression of spiritual practice.

During the summer months the kitchen produces six meals a day, every day — three meals for seventy students acting as staff and three meals for the seventy overnight guests. Many guests are drawn to Tassajara by the gourmet, healthy vegetarian fare. Here are some of the values that exemplify how this kitchen serves as a model for work as a spiritual practice:

Clarity of activity. Working in the Tassajara kitchen, it is almost always clear what needs to be done next. The daily menus and the next day's menus are posted on a corkboard. Under each meal is a detailed list of ingredients and how each dish is to be prepared. Everyone can see the larger plan and the details of the plan. The assistant cook knows just when each ingredient is required by the cooks. The cooks are generally cooking the next meal as well as preparing several meals ahead of time.

High degree of organization. Every knife, utensil, pot, and pan has a very specific place in the kitchen. Areas are neatly organized and labeled. Processes are very clear — when leftover food is put away, it is always dated. Sponges are also left standing upright so that they can air-dry. Knives are always cleaned, dried, and put away after use. Counters are cleaned, and floors are swept after each meal.

Regular rhythms. The flow of each day is very predictable. Meals always appear at the same time. Other regular schedules include planning, preparation, cleanup, and rituals. There is a clear structure and schedule each day. Within this structure, anything can happen — people get sick, potatoes get burned, knives need sharpening. The schedule allows for a tremendous amount of freedom and creativity within a clear and disciplined framework.

Straightforward flow of information. The head cook works with the management team to formulate a budget and is responsible for ordering food. The head cook meets regularly with the cooks, the assistant cook, and the preparation crew. The cooks, in conjunction with the head cook, plan the menus. The assistant cook runs the day-to-day kitchen, acting as the link between all parts of the kitchen — directing assignments and general flow, as well as anticipating and solving problems.

Equal valuing of every job. The head cook buys the vegetables. The assistant cook decides and communicates who will cut them. The cook for the day determines how the vegetables will be cut, and the crew cuts them. The cook uses the vegetables to prepare a dish. Every step is equally important.

Clear roles. Every role is defined, from purchasing the food, planning meals, budgeting, daily assignments, cutting and preparing, to cleaning up. Each person knows his or her role and the role of everyone else in the kitchen.

Work as spiritual practice. There is an understanding that working in the kitchen is a means to practice mindfulness, awareness, and compassion. People are assigned roles not primarily because of their cooking skills but because it is determined that the kitchen will provide a useful atmosphere for their personal and spiritual growth. There is a dual bottom line: 1) producing healthy, tasty food presented in a way that is simple and creative; 2) building character in the people working in the kitchen. There are no conversations, no small talk. The only talking is in relation to the tasks at hand.

Cross training. There are regular opportunities to work in other positions. The cooks often bake, and the bakers often cook. On the cooks' days off, crew members fill in.

Clear expectations. Everyone has a clear vision of the anticipated quality of the food and the workmanship — at all levels, from how food is prepared, to how the counters are cleaned, to how the food is served.

Regular, measurable outcomes. There is regular feedback from students and from guests at every meal. People express what they like and don't like about each meal, the combinations of food, the seasonings, the presentation. The cooks often eat in the dining room alongside the guests to experience firsthand the results of their labor. The cooks then address what worked and didn't work well and incorporate this information into planning future meals.

Working together and separately. Although nearly every aspect of work in the kitchen is done individually, it is part of a group effort. Each person works alone chopping vegetables. Then a cook uses these vegetables when creating the meal.

Regular job rotation. No one stays in any position for more than a year or two. Generally, even head cook is a one-year position.

Being stretched to achieve. Kitchen assignments are not based primarily on levels of skills and experience. Though skills and experience are taken into account, the primary factor in determining kitchen roles is based on what roles are deemed to help a person to grow.

Ritual. The word *ritual* can be defined as activity performed for a higher purpose. Kitchen work at Tassajara is viewed as meditation in action. Each morning the kitchen crew sits one period of meditation with everyone in the community and then leaves the meditation hall to begin work in the kitchen. The crew begins working at 5:00

A.M., aware that others are still meditating. Every morning at 6:30 the assistant cook rings a small bell in the kitchen. Everyone stops whatever he or she is doing and gathers around an altar located inside the kitchen, right next to the main cutting table. The head cook offers incense. Everyone bows to the altar, then chants together. Everyone bows again to the altar, then bows to each other. The group then gathers in a small circle, and there is time for announcements, for welcoming any new people into the kitchen, and for addressing the overall plan for the day. With ritual taking place in the midst of the kitchen environment, all activity begins to feel like ritual.

Many or all these practices can be applied to a variety of work environments, whether in the office, the classroom, or the operating room. Choose a practice that applies to your situation, either by yourself or with a group. Experiment. Play. See what happens. Learn from what works and from what doesn't.

QUESTIONS FOR DAILY PRACTICE

- What is your model of the ideal environment for integrating work practice and spiritual practice?

- What lessons from the Tassajara kitchen could you integrate into your work life?

- What rituals do you have in your workplace?

- What rituals can be added?

- How can you apply the practices outlined in this chapter to your work environment and to your life?

IMPERMANENCE

During the summer when I was director of Tassajara cold drinks and leftover sweets were served every afternoon to students and guests. One very hot August afternoon, shortly after the tea break, I was informed by one of our staff members that a student was feeling sick and needed to be replaced in the kitchen. A few minutes later I was told that another student was not feeling well. Then someone came running up to me saying that a guest had suddenly become very ill and was having trouble breathing. Fortunately, two of the guests at Tassajara were physicians. One of them began asking what had been served for tea that afternoon and discovered that a student had prepared a special tea that day — made from fresh elderberries picked from the nearby hillside. This physician knew that the bark and leaves of elderberries were quite poisonous and that we needed to find and evacuate everyone who had drunk the elderberry tea. We discovered ten people who were seriously ill.

Tassajara is in the middle of a wilderness area, two hours from the nearest hospital. There was an emergency helicopter site located on top of a hill protruding from the east end of the valley. I immediately went to the one telephone in Tassajara (a crank phone that required being connected to an operator in Salinas) and called the emergency helicopter number. I told the man who answered the phone that several people were severely ill and that we needed a helicopter flown in immediately. He responded by asking me how to get to Tassajara via helicopter. I could not believe I was hearing this question.

I felt that my senses had become completely open. I was watching and listening for clues and information about what to do and how to respond to this situation. About forty-five minutes later I could hear the sound of a helicopter approaching. I ran to the central part of Tassajara Valley to catch the attention of the helicopter pilot. I signaled for him to try to land in the center of the valley; I hoped to avoid having to carry sick people up a steep and narrow path to the top of the hill. As the helicopter descended into the valley, the wind thrown off by its rotor struck the steep valley walls, making it impossible to land. I began to run toward the hilltop helicopter site to direct the pilot where to land.

Four people were needed to carry each of six sick people to the top of the hill and help load them into the helicopter. This was all that this helicopter could accommodate. The other four people, who were in slightly better condition, were driven to the hospital. I stood next to the helicopter as its large side door was slid shut and its motor revved. My heart sank as the helicopter slowly slid off the side of the steep hill and quickly plummeted toward the bottom of the valley, before swooping upward again. Everyone completely recovered.

It seems as though we have no choice but to act as though the world is permanent, solid, and predictable, and, at the same time, we must realize that everything around us is impermanent, fluid, and unpredictable. If we go too far toward believing in permanence, we will be thrown when something unexpected happens. If we lean too far toward a belief in impermanence, we may fall into the trap of not setting clear goals, not achieving what is within our potential, and living irresponsibly. This can be a way of protecting ourselves from failure or sometimes of protecting ourselves from success.

The secret of successful business practice and of life practice is finding the balance between control and letting go, between understanding that though little is within our control, we must act with complete responsibility. It is vital that we define our own paths, that we act with integrity, that we set clear goals for ourselves, and that we define and live by our life's purpose. At the same time we must be prepared to change directions, to face whatever may come our way. You might say that the purpose of Zen and the purpose of business practice is to develop an open, flexible mind, a mind that can deal with a world that is both solid and completely impermanent.

The great Zen teacher Dogen said that our lives are like being in a boat on a river. We have no control over the river. The river flows regardless of our actions. Our job is to take care of our boat and to steer it. As our boat floats down the river of life we must be prepared for whatever comes our way.

Impermanence teaches us that nothing stays the same. Everything changes from moment to moment. Nothing in our business or work lives is stagnant. Our response to the fact of impermanence can be to feel stress and fear, or we can understand that because everything changes we can relax and feel the wonder of not knowing what will happen next. Understanding impermanence can give us confidence, peace, and joy.

QUESTIONS FOR DAILY PRACTICE

- In what ways do you fear change at work? Where does this fear come from? What might happen?

- In what ways does change at work bring you comfort and joy?

- What aspects of your work are within your control?

- What aspects of your work are outside your control?

- How do you balance control and letting go in your work life?

- How do you tend to respond to change? When do you feel fear? When do you relish change?

LISTENING TO YOUR CLEAR,
QUIET VOICE

I think of myself as having been asleep for most of my child-hood. In high school my goal was to get good grades while learning as little as possible. I was successful at both these goals. While at college, I developed a passion for learning and became particularly interested in studying psychology and Eastern and Western mysticism. I took every class that Rutgers had to offer in this realm — classes in religion, psychology, philosophy, and liter-ature. I also began reading books about Zen and humanistic psy-chology by Alan Watts, Carl Jung, Abraham Maslow, and others. The more I studied the more I realized that I wanted not just to read about spirituality — I wanted to practice it.

I had heard from a friend in New Jersey about a program in San Francisco called the Humanist Institute. It was a small com-munity that offered classes in meditation, dream work, and the study and practice of Eastern and Western mysticism. The institute had a small, full-time program, and a group sat meditation each morning and evening. I took a one-year leave of absence from Rut-gers and headed west.

I was twenty-two when I first arrived in San Francisco. I supported myself by doing part-time office work in downtown businesses. Every day I took the bus from my apartment in the Haight Ashbury district to and from work. Every morning and every afternoon the bus would pass by the corner of Page and Laguna streets, where there was a large red brick building. I had been told that this building was the Zen Center headquarters, which I had heard of through reading *The Tassajara Bread Book*. I was drawn by the book's emphasis on bringing attention to the inner life and the quality of one's being through the simple activity of baking bread.

One day, in the spring of 1974, I decided to get off the bus. I walked into the building on Page Street, the Zen Center headquarters. I was struck by how clean, quiet, orderly, and comfortable everything felt. There was a wonderful smell, probably a blend of incense and baking bread. Several people were working in the office. They were not particularly friendly, nor were they unfriendly, but they gave me lots of space to look around and ask questions. The artwork on the walls was amazing, a combination of ancient and modern Buddhist images that were alive, turbulent, and calm, all at the same time. I could feel the intention and values of bridging the inner life and outward actions. I immediately felt that I had stepped onto a path that was vitally important for me.

Listening deeply and carefully is a skill I practice regularly as Brush Dance CEO. Much of my daily business life at Brush Dance, from working with my staff to evaluating overall strategy, revolves around listening to what is not obvious: How is my staff feeling? Are people motivated, working together, in sync with the disciplines and directions agreed upon? Are changes required in defining jobs or in increasing or decreasing staff? Is this the right time to experiment with some new product categories or to pursue some new channels of distribution? What are my salespeople trying to tell us? Of course I am regularly evaluating all the "hard" information —

financial reports, trends, and ratios — but I see this information as a lens helping me to see more clearly what cannot be quantified, what doesn't fit into any neat package.

By watching and listening carefully, the most important decisions can emerge, ones that just might keep the business on the current course, signal a time to make a subtle shift, or point out the need for a radical change. When I look closely at Brush Dance, all three of these types of adjustments are constantly taking place. We hold our course by understanding that our strength is making spiritual ideas accessible. This is something I think we do better than other companies, it is something we feel passion for, and it represents a growing need in the marketplace. We make minor shifts and adjustments in our staffing, in our product offerings, and in how we market and distribute. And we sometimes conduct radical experiments or make major changes in overall strategy. Our clear, quiet voice can be our best friend and greatest teacher.

Zen practice often speaks of our having a "monkey mind," a mind that is noisy and jumps from thought to thought, barking our plans and worries in a loud voice. And we each have a "wide mind," a mind that is calm and quiet, that looks at everything from a composed, open perspective. This wide mind speaks with a voice so quiet it can be difficult to hear. Our explanations for why we make certain choices are the stories we tell ourselves, while underneath the noise and the stories the important decisions are made.

QUESTIONS FOR DAILY PRACTICE

- When do you hear your quiet, subtle voice — during meditation, while driving, while falling asleep?

- Which of your stories and myths explain your major life decisions?

- What does your voice tell you about the work you are doing now?

- When you listen to your voice of satisfaction, what does it say? How does it sound?

- When you listen to your voice of dissatisfaction, what can you learn?

RADICAL VIEW OF LIFE,
RADICAL VIEW OF BUSINESS

"Radical: arising from or going to the root or source;
fundamental; basic."
— Webster's Dictionary

When my son was a teenager he once said to me, "Dad, I just don't get it. Why do people spend so much time doing what they don't really enjoy, just to get ahead or to make money? Don't they get it? Don't they see that we are all going to die?" I thought this was a great observation and a great question.

Integrating Zen practice with business practice is a "radical" choice — radical in the sense of returning to the values and way of life that are most basic and fundamental to human beings. A monk takes a radical view of life, choosing to return to the root, the most basic level of human existence, focusing on the inner life, on living simply, and fostering self-knowledge and compassion for others as a way to change the world. A monk lives a very simple, very basic life. A monk shuns the ordinary assumptions about success and failure. A monk, through his or her choices, makes a statement and sets an example to the world regarding the importance of focusing on what is most basic to human existence and satisfaction. A monk lives and operates outside society's definitions and at the same time understands that there is no escaping these definitions.

An entrepreneur or any small businessperson takes a radical view of business, choosing to return to the root, the most basic form of commerce, of meeting the needs of people and creating a response that is direct and basic. An entrepreneur defines success and failure for herself. An entrepreneur sets an example to the world regarding focusing on what is most basic and important to business. An entrepreneur works outside society's definitions and at the same time understands that there is no escaping society's definitions. Being joyful, honest, open, and vulnerable in business is a radical idea. I believe that there are no accidents, that it is no accident that we find ourselves in whatever work situation we have chosen. There are many "radical" similarities between Zen practice and business practice:

- They are both challenging, and with each challenge comes the possibility of achievement and satisfaction.

- They are both fraught with possibilities, unknowns, and adventure. Anything could happen. There are no limits.

- They both draw on inner and outer practices. How we experience and perceive the world is vitally important. Both provide the chance to work on our inner lives, to expose patterns, and to develop character.

- They are both outward practices, aimed at making a difference in the world. Zen practice makes a political, social, and economic statement. A business makes a political, social, and economic statement.

- They both provide an opportunity to affect people on a local, community, and global level.

- They are both disciplines with clear guidelines and practices.

- They both possess a magical and mystical quality when practiced wholeheartedly.

Zen practice may appear radical from the outside. For people practicing, however, it is a simple and direct way of life. As in business practice, there are no clear rules, path, or map. Zen isn't something you take down from the shelf and then put on like clothing. Your *life* is the practice. This returning to the most fundamental description of practicing Zen is what makes it such a radical practice, a return to an immediate way of life.

From the outside being an entrepreneur may also appear to be a radical choice. But I believe that the definition of *entrepreneur* is much broader than "someone who starts a business." It is much more a radical way of thinking and living in the world — learning directly from each experience, each problem, each person that we meet.

QUESTIONS FOR DAILY PRACTICE

- What defines you as radical?

- In what ways are you a "monk" — in your intentions, lifestyle, and daily activities?

- In what ways are you an entrepreneur? What have you begun? What do you oversee?

- When you envision your ideal work situation, what kinds of actions are you performing? How do you interact with people? How do you use your gifts and talents?

ACCOMPLISHING MORE BY DOING LESS

I was surprised, honored, and intimidated when I was asked to be the Tassajara summer baker. I had some baking experience, having spent a winter in the Tassajara kitchen, but I had never made the quantities and varieties of breads that were expected of someone in this position. Also, the Tassajara baker has the reputation to uphold of making terrific bread. Each day the baker's job is to make twenty-five to thirty each of three to four different kinds of bread, a total of one hundred to one hundred and twenty loaves, all completely from scratch. Bread was served at student and guest meals and was also offered for sale each day for guests to take home.

For the first two months, this was the most physically strenuous job I had ever had. My days began at 5:00 A.M., and the last batch of bread came out of the oven at about 4:00 P.M. After dinner I would research and plan the breads for the next day, often meeting with the guest cooks to confirm the menus. During the workday I was mixing and kneading by hand forty- to fifty-pound batches of bread, measuring, cutting, and shaping loaves, baking loaves in three different ovens, and orchestrating all this in the middle of an active, bustling kitchen. After completing the baking in the late afternoon, I generally collapsed, my muscles aching, my body hot and exhausted. I ate dinner and then began planning the next day's menu and recipes.

By the middle of the summer, something clicked. Mixing a batch that had taken me forty minutes in the early summer now took me less than ten minutes. It seemed, suddenly, that very little effort was required. Whereas I had struggled with the kneading process in early summer, by midsummer it seemed almost effortless. My body had learned how to mix and knead these large and heavy batches of bread without expending much effort.

I learned, over and over, as the Tassajara bread baker, that the less I did, the better the bread came out. The secret to making tasty bread was to plan ahead, use good ingredients, and let the bread do the work. This was an amazing discovery!

My second job after graduating from business school was with a $10 million distributor of recycled paper. I came on as the company was gearing up for explosive growth. Everyone worked really hard, people didn't take lunch breaks, and nearly everyone worked on weekends. I noticed that the harder people worked, the less seemed to be accomplished. Soon after I started working for this company, I was asked to work on a Saturday. I spent a Saturday afternoon in a meeting with the company's president in which very little was achieved. I made it clear from that point on that I could not work on weekends, except for very clearly stated projects.

I contacted one of my business mentors about dealing with the company culture. He suggested that I clearly state that my rule is to have dinner every evening with my family. I let my boss and my co-workers know about this rule, and not only was it not questioned, but I believe it was also respected. And I actually did have dinner every night with my wife and two children. The work that needed to get done was completed without my needing to work late or on weekends.

Accomplishment has much more to do with focus than with time and effort. We can get more done in a few focused hours than in many days of not being focused. There is a story of a consultant engineer who is called in on an emergency to find a crack in a large oil tank system. The consultant spends about five minutes looking over this complicated system and within a few minutes determines exactly where the leak is. He billed the oil company $10,000 for his services. The company contested that there must be a mistake; how could he charge so much money for five minutes of work? The consultant replied that he had spent many years honing his skills, which enabled him to determine, in very little time, where the leak was. He charged for what he accomplished, not for how long the job took.

At Brush Dance's inception I was responsible for every aspect of the business — strategy, sales and marketing, accounting, and even wrapping and shipping the packages. As the business grew I hired people to take on specific roles, but I continued to manage key areas of sales and product development. Today all the departments are run by managers who have more skill and experience than I do. My key role in the company is to be present, to provide guidance and support. I feel much like I did as a baker — the less I do the better the bread comes out.

QUESTIONS FOR DAILY PRACTICE

- Can you remember a time when you accomplished more by doing less?

- How do you balance doing and not doing in your work?

- How much time do you spend at work performing activities that are not really necessary? How can you change this?

- What major changes and transformations have occurred in your work? How did these come about?

THE POWER OF INTENTION

Beings are numberless. I vow to save them.
Delusions are inexhaustible; I vow to end them.
Dharma gates are boundless; I vow to enter them.
Buddha's way is unsurpassable; I vow to become it.

These vows, which are chanted at the end of Zen lectures, express the fundamental intentions of Zen practice. They elevate our day-to-day activities and provide a larger context in which to live. Though these statements appear lofty and impossible, they act as a target, a set of goals to strive for, a direction in which to point our intentions. Though Zen is very practical by nature, it also has a way of challenging us to aim very high and not to be limited by conventional ideas of what is possible. Expressing these intentions makes ordinary activity extraordinary.

Sometimes as I am preparing for my workday I chant a variation of the Buddhist lecture chant:

The needs and problems of people are endless; I vow to find
*   ways to meet their needs and solve these problems.*
Daily work problems are inexhaustible; I vow to solve them.
Opportunities for practicing and creating intimacy at work
*   are boundless: I vow to discover them.*
Opportunities for inspiring others and transforming our
*   world are everywhere: I vow to act on them.*

The vow to meet the needs of people. The essence of Brush Dance is to create products that help people see the world a little differently, to open people to new ways of thinking, and to help people communicate directly and compassionately. Focusing on the needs of people is basic to all business.

The vow to solve all problems. We are never finished solving problems. There is no starting or ending point. The moment one issue is resolved, it is time to focus on the next one. Every problem presents an opportunity. Every opportunity presents additional problems and challenges.

Practicing and creating intimacy at work. Everywhere we look there are problems, pain, and suffering. At each moment we have the chance to be present, to practice at work, and to be fully ourselves. Nothing is stopping us from being open, honest, and vulnerable at work and from meeting others at a deep and intimate level.

Opportunities for inspiring others and transforming our world. There is no end to what we can discover about ourselves. Our bodies, minds, and spirit have no boundaries. Our work provides endless opportunities for self-discovery and growth and for inspiring others. By deeply touching the people we come into contact with at work we can help the world become a place of generosity and peace and move it away from greed and conflict.

The concept of making a vow, or holding a very deep intention, is quite foreign to most business environments. This practice seems heavy and serious, especially in contrast to the usual commitments people have regarding their work. Generally, making money to support ourselves and our families is a key motivator, usually followed by our desire to do a good job or to do something useful and fulfilling.

The word *vow* is primarily internal, tapping into the deeper stream of our lives, and is not generally used in relation to our changing, external circumstances. A vow is a promise, a statement of intention and of commitment that we make to ourselves. Although they are internal, sometimes we make our vows more public by sharing them with our spouse, family, colleagues, or closest friends.

QUESTIONS FOR DAILY PRACTICE

- What are your vows and deepest, most fundamental intentions at work?

- What do you want to accomplish during your brief time on this planet?

- What kind of work do you most enjoy?

- What kind of work do you believe you were meant to do?

- What are your vows in terms of meeting people, addressing problems, looking for opportunities for growth, and for self-discovery at work?

WHAT DO YOU WANT?
WHAT DO YOU HAVE TO DO TO GET IT?
CAN YOU PAY THE PRICE?

Harry Roberts was a friend and teacher of mine while I lived at Zen Center's Green Gulch Farm. He was fond of saying that life is very simple — all you have to do is answer three questions: 1) What do you want? 2) What do you have to do to get it? and 3) Can you pay the price? After stating these questions he would usually laugh heartily, saying, yeah, real simple; most people don't ever ask themselves the first question.

Harry was trained as a medicine man in the Yurok Indian tradition. He had been a cowboy and a farmer and was a PhD agronomist who designed the gardens at the University of California, Berkeley. Harry used to say that a primary difference between American Indian culture and Western culture is that Indians believed that each person is born with a particular skill and strength, that there is a primary reason for each person to be on the planet. The responsibility of parents is to provide opportunities for each child to discover his or her purpose and mission, to discover the kind of talents he or she was born to express. Indians believed that by careful observation, you could usually see by age three what a person's lifelong work was likely to be. Harry often said that it is vital for each person not only to discover her song but also to sing it.

What do you want? This is the simplest question, and the most difficult. What is really important to you? What is the purpose of your life? What is your true intention? How do you want to spend your time? What do you want to accomplish? What has meaning for you? What do you want from your work life? What do you want from your relationships? Where is your passion? What kinds of activities do you find most satisfying? Spending time with any one of these questions can change your life.

What do you have to do to get what you want? Once you have answered this question, it is time to determine what you need to do to get what you want. What skills do you need, what training or schooling is required? What steps do you need to take? What do you already have, and what is needed?

These questions make me think of a woman who tells her friend that she really wants to be a lawyer, but she is forty-two years old. Because of her age, she doesn't think she can fulfill this goal. She says it will take her three years to complete law school and that she would be forty-five by the time she finishes. Her friend asks her, "How old will you be in three years if you don't go to law school?"

Harry used to say that everything comes with a price. Can you pay the price? Choosing something means not choosing something else. Choosing what you want and laying out a plan require that you then take the steps needed, do the work, or go through whatever difficulties you are likely to confront. Every choice comes with a price that begins with risks. This question puts your resolve to the test — once you know what you want and what you have to do to get it, are you willing to risk failure, are you willing to give up other paths?

A few years ago, when my daughter was fourteen, we had a

conversation while in our driveway, finishing our smoothies. At the time I was trying to formulate a vision of what I wanted to accomplish. I said to her, "I wonder what I'll be when I grow up?" Carol pondered the question for a few moments and said *she* might want to be a photographer. Then she asked me what a photographer does, how they make money and how much they make. Then she said she might want to be a writer, or perhaps a teacher. Then she looked over at me. I was thinking. I said that I could imagine being a college professor or a writer or perhaps a therapist. We were both feeling relaxed and content, just talking and dreaming about the future. We were connected by the question, by facing the unknown together.

QUESTIONS FOR DAILY PRACTICE

- What do you want? Really?

- What is most important in your life?

- What do you have to do to get it? What is involved? What does the path in front of you look like?

- Can you pay the price? What does it take to make this decision, to make this change?

NO OTHER TRUTH

If you can't find the truth right where you are,
where do you expect to find it?
— Dogen

Harry used to tell a story about how his teacher chose the students he would accept. Many more students wanted to work with him than he could accommodate. His teacher would say to the student, "Go find ten different kinds of plants." If the student walked away and began looking for plants, she was not accepted. The person who did not leave but instead looked down, standing right where he was, was accepted as a student.

Brush Dance was founded as an environmental products mail-order catalog. We were one of the first companies in the United States to make wrapping paper and greeting cards from recycled paper. We began in 1989 with two wrapping paper designs and a few greeting cards and did a test mailing of a one-page brochure to five thousand individuals. The response was encouraging. In 1990 we produced a sixteen-page catalog, with a variety of wrapping papers, greeting cards, and a few gifts, all made from recycled paper. Again, the response was encouraging.

In 1990 we began to be contacted by stores and by representatives who sold to stores. We started to see that perhaps we were not a mail-order company but a wholesale company. Two large mail-order catalogs contacted us and placed orders for our wrapping paper that were larger than all our individual orders combined. Though the tests we conducted as a mail-order company got positive results, it appeared that to grow as a mail-order business would require large amounts of capital. I concluded that growing as a wholesale company could be achieved by ramping up more slowly and would require much lower up-front costs. Most important, though most of our energy and resources were being aimed at selling to individuals through our catalog, most of our revenue was coming from selling to large catalog companies and stores.

With this understanding we began to transform the company. For example, as a mail-order business we wanted to offer cards in a variety of sizes. As a wholesale company selling to stores, we needed to offer cards in a standard size to fit into store displays. Instead of marketing to individuals we began to focus on stores and other mail-order catalogs.

Another surprising finding was that people were not drawn to our products because they were made from recycled paper. The feedback we were getting was that it was the spiritual nature of our words and the way we combined powerful words with beautiful designs that were unique. People appreciated that our products were environmentally friendly, but only after they made their purchase. People purchased our products because they were moved by the words and images.

For Brush Dance, discovering that the company was a wholesale producer of products with meaningful words and not a mail-order environmental products company was like looking down at our feet to see who we really were.

The starting point for integrating Zen practice with your work life is to fully accept and take stock of where you are in your work life right now. You can't begin where you want to be or hope to be. Regrets are not productive. You are where you are. You learn from what is right in front of you. There is no other starting point, no other truth.

QUESTIONS FOR DAILY PRACTICE

- Where are you in your work life trajectory? Where have you come from, and where do you see yourself going?

- What are your strengths and weaknesses?

- What do you bring to your work that is unique?

- What are the benefits and advantages to your situation, experiences, and talents?

- What can you learn from where you are in your work life?

- What do you like about your work? What do you want more of?

- What do you dislike about your work? What do you want less of?

TAKING THE BUSYNESS OUT OF BUSINESS

When hot, just be hot. When cold, be thoroughly cold.
— Zen expression

When my father was dying from cancer we took him from the hospital to his home, where he had lived for twenty years. This was not an easy decision, particularly for my mother. I was a young Zen student, on leave from my work as a horse farmer. We didn't know how much longer my father would live, and I didn't know how long I would be able to stay before having to go back to Green Gulch. The experience of being with someone who is dying is filled with intensity and unknowns. How do you give the person hope, open the door to the possibility of change and healing and at the same time help the person prepare to die?

During this time a visiting nurse came to the house each day. The first day she came she threw away the dying flowers that were next to my father's bed and replaced them with fresh ones. The next day she cut my father's fingernails, which had become quite long. While I was busy struggling with the big questions of life and death, time and impermanence, the nurse was taking care of what was right at hand, dead flowers and overgrown nails.

There is a famous Zen story about a young monk who sees an older monk sweeping the grounds of the temple and says to him, "Too busy!" He is implying that the older monk should be practicing meditation and not working. The older monk says to the

171

younger monk, "There is someone here who is not too busy." The teacher is pointing out that although he is sweeping and not meditating, this does not mean he is busy. Sweeping, or any activity, can be a way to practice mindfulness.

One of the primary challenges in our work lives, and in our lives in general, is to find the "one who is not busy." The definition of *busy* is "crowded with activity." Activity itself has nothing to do with being busy. It is possible to be "busy" while practicing meditation — if what we are doing is being caught by our thoughts, plans, and worries. How can we be present for what we are doing? When sitting, just sit. When walking, just walk. When speaking on the phone, just speak on the phone. When making a business presentation, just make a business presentation. How can we find the part of us that is "not busy" no matter what we are doing?

In our culture being "busy" has become a virtue. We don't have time just to relax, to do nothing. We rarely have time for socializing or for being with friends. I often hear people say that they don't have a regular meditation practice because they don't have time. This is like a carpenter saying that he is so busy working that he doesn't have time to sharpen his saw.

At work, we often feel we need to look and feel busy all the time. I notice that even as the owner and CEO, I often feel the same pressure to appear busy. The busier we are, the more important, the more needed we feel. The more overscheduled we are, the higher our status seems. Driving home from work today I laughed in amazement at how many people were talking on the phone as they were driving, how many were talking on the phone as they were walking.

It is such a relief to give up the idea of needing to appear busy. It is okay to complete a task or project and have nothing to do, to rest, to take a break, to celebrate a completion or accomplishment before going on to the next task. After all, the sun rises and sets each day, regardless of how much we accomplish.

Stephen Covey, in his book *First Things First*, developed a chart to help us prioritize and manage our time. On one side of a four-boxed grid are the labels "important" and "unimportant." On the bottom of the grid are "urgent" and "not urgent." The chart forms four quadrants: important and urgent, important and not urgent, unimportant and not urgent, unimportant and urgent. Covey asserts that we all need to pay attention to spending less time doing what is unimportant and urgent and more time doing what is important and not urgent. This quadrant includes long-term planning and a sense of practice.

I think that another dimension is needed to make Covey's chart more complete and useful. The labels in the chart I would suggest are "intimacy" on one side and "impermanence" on the other. These words would appear in all four quadrants. This is the spiritual dimension of our work, in which we recognize how short our lives are and in which we open ourselves enough to make real connections and to establish real intimacy. The spiritual dimension of time requires more than good time management. It requires that we discover in ourselves "the one who is not busy."

QUESTIONS FOR DAILY PRACTICE

- How important is it to appear busy in your work?

- What happens if you are not "busy"?

- Experiment with stopping, relaxing, enjoying, and relishing a sense of accomplishment at the completion of a project.

- Can you lose yourself in your activity, without judging or watching yourself?

HAVING A TEACHER OR MENTOR

When Brush Dance was just getting off the ground, I went to see Paul Hawken, founder and CEO of Smith & Hawken, for some business advice. At that time, Smith & Hawken was at the pinnacle of its success. It was a thriving $50 million mail-order gardening supplies catalog, growing quickly and getting plenty of media and investor attention. Paul had a beautiful corner office and was surrounded by a vibrant and engaged staff.

Paul told me three things that have stayed with me all these years. First, he said that he does not take anything for granted. He often looks around his office, sees his employees and his many products, and realizes that it could all easily disappear at any time. Paul then told me that he started a mail-order catalog business instead of a different kind of business so that he would never have to go to trade shows or collect money from customers. These were two things he had done in previous businesses that he did not want to do again. And last, Paul explained to me that the mail-order business was a lot like gambling. The image he painted was of the mail-order business being like standing at an open window with your arms filled with money. You throw all the money you have out the window and hope that more money comes back in than you threw out.

I have always had several teachers and mentors, both as a Zen student and as the founder of Brush Dance. Rudy, my first business mentor, was instrumental in helping me improve and develop my business plan, and his support gave me the confidence to launch the business. As the founder and CEO of a growing business I have found it invaluable to have an engaged board of directors, a bright and accessible lawyer and accountant, and a variety of mentors who could help me with personal issues, problem solving, and negotiations.

I meet several times a year with a successful businesswoman I was introduced to through being a member of the Social Venture Network. SVN is a group of business leaders who are engaged in combining business and social responsibility. She speaks with me openly and directly about how my strengths and weaknesses, my habits and patterns, and my vision are intertwined with the path and success of Brush Dance. She taught me that the more I walked my own path the likelier it would be that Brush Dance would fulfill its mission in the world.

I also enjoy my lunches with an old friend from when we lived at Zen Center, who went on to become a successful businessman. He spent twenty years growing software companies and then became a high-level corporate business manager. He advises me on Brush Dance marketing and financial strategies and helps me in working with my board and investors.

Every six weeks I have dinner with a childhood friend, during which we mentor each other. He worked as a psychotherapist for many years and is now a successful businessman. We each present the most pressing problems of the day. We listen, support each other, challenge each other's assumptions, and offer direction. Being mentored is an important way to learn, to grow, and to receive invaluable perspective.

For many years I believed that someone knew and could tell me the path that Brush Dance needed to take to be successful (or the path that I needed to take to be satisfied or successful). I have learned that it is possible to be overly dependent on what others have to say and also possible not to listen enough to what others have to say. Another paradox is that the more I cultivate my relationships with a variety of mentors, the more I learn to listen to myself. I have discovered that the advice, knowledge, and guidance I receive from my mentors is invaluable. I listen, weigh options, and evaluate everything they suggest. And I have discovered that ultimately I must take everything I know into consideration to make the ultimate decision.

I also find the role of mentoring to be extremely valuable. Not only does advising others allow me to feel that I am giving back, after having received so much, but I also occasionally have the experience of listening to what I am saying and thinking, "That's pretty good advice — that's something I may want to listen to."

List your mentors or potential mentors. Make a list of the people who have helped you on your path and write why you are grateful to each. Call potential mentors and schedule meetings — people like to help, to offer advice, to mentor. Make a point of visiting with spiritual teachers in your area — go to lectures or one-day sittings.

QUESTIONS FOR DAILY PRACTICE

- What mentors have been most important to you in your work life?

- How have they helped you?

- What kinds of mentors would be useful to have in your life now?

INTERDEPENDENCE

O ne of my business school professors at New York University spoke of starting twenty-six different businesses during his career. His classes in small business development and entrepreneurship were always well attended. One day he advised, "Always start your business by yourself; avoid the headaches of having to work with another person, dividing responsibilities, ownership, and power."

But he then went on to say of the twenty-six different businesses he started, not one of them was started by him alone. He always had at least one partner. "None of us has the skills and talents it takes to start and run a business. We cannot be good at everything. We need the skills and talents of others to successfully run a business."

Nearly everything that I have done in business has involved the help of other people. When I started Brush Dance I had no money. I initially borrowed some from my family and friends. As the business grew I sold stock to family and friends, and then to friends of friends. I brought together groups of friends to help me decide what to name the business. I consulted with mentors regarding product development and distribution. The business depends on artists to create our designs. We license the words that we use on our cards and calendars from teachers and authors. We rely on our salespeople across the country to show and sell our products to store buyers. We rely on our printers and vendors, who are spread out from northern California to China and Korea. We depend on the owners and workers in stores to purchase and display our products, and we rely on customers to buy our products.

We are clearly neither independent nor dependent. We can't do it on our own, and at the same time we must trust our vision and inner voice. The idea for beginning Brush Dance was "my" idea, arising from many other ideas and from what I learned from numerous teachers and mentors. When the idea came to me it was as though I had no choice but to begin this business. Yet the idea came from watching another business.

When I was a manager at Conservatree Paper Company, one of my largest customers was a mail-order catalog, Earth Care Paper, a company selling greeting cards and wrapping paper made from recycled paper. I watched this company explode from being a mom-and-pop organization to becoming a $5 million company. I didn't think the designs on their products were that special. They were primarily nature drawings, and I thought that I could find artists who could make much more interesting and compelling designs. That is where "my" idea originated — I began by taking someone else's idea and thought about improving it. Then the business evolved to meet the changing demands of the marketplace. I now see many companies that are taking Brush Dance's successes and growing their own businesses by improving on or changing what we initiated.

From the moment we are born we are both on our own and dependent on others. No one can breathe for us or think for us. Yet we need our parents for food, protection, and nurturing. Everything about our lives is interdependent — neither independent nor dependent.

QUESTIONS FOR DAILY PRACTICE

- Who supports your work?

- What supports and affects your work life?

- How do your family and friends support your work?

- Draw a circle with you in the center. On the outside of the circle name the various things and people that support you. Now draw a wheel with you as one of the spokes. What is in the center of your wheel? What are the other spokes?

SUCCESS IS HIGHLY OVERRATED

Those who have never made mistakes
have never made anything.

Several years ago I was invited to speak at a "Business and Spirit" conference. The topic that I was asked to address was "the dark night of the soul in business." The organizers of this conference knew that I had had some difficult and humbling business experiences. I spoke about how difficult it was to grow a business, the constant concerns about cash flow and the challenge of almost always being on the edge of survival. I told the story of the day when Brush Dance's cash flow was so bad that, when I looked at what we owed our printers, artists, sales reps, and employees, the entire room began to spin. I felt physically ill and sat at my desk and cried.

The irony is that I had no idea then just how bad things were really going to become. The following year things became much worse. It was as though each difficult experience was preparing me for the next, even more difficult experience.

There is a Zen story about four horses. The first horse starts to run when it sees the shadow of the driver's whip. The second horse starts running when it feels the whip just touching its hairs. The third horse runs when it feels the whip against its skin; and the fourth horse doesn't run until it feels the pain of the whip in its bones. Of course, we all want to be the first horse, the horse that is the quickest and most clever. None of us wants to be the last horse, the horse that is slowest to learn.

I have certainly always yearned to be like the first horse. Unfortunately, I have often felt much more like the fourth horse. I think of myself as learning very slowly, but learning well. I have to read things over and over until I really understand them. I've also noticed that my particular style of learning is physical — I need to actually do something, to experience something, to learn a new skill or concept.

Brush Dance embarked on an Internet strategy at precisely the wrong time. In March of 2000 a group of investors wrote a check to Brush Dance for $1 million as the seed money to fund the development of what was to be a major body-mind-spirit business. In April the Internet bubble began showing signs of bursting. Of course, at that time, no one knew that it was a bubble. Many people believed that this was a temporary stumble. We moved ahead fully with our plans, including hiring a CEO to run the Internet business, moving to a large and expensive facility in Mill Valley, and increasing staffing from twelve to twenty-four people (many quite expensive Internet employees).

By February of 2001 the bubble had completely burst. The company had spent the $1 million and an additional $1.5 million in loans. Nearly all investment money had stopped flowing. On February 19 we were completely out of funds, and our investors announced that they would not be investing or loaning additional funds. The CEO we had hired to run the Internet business informed me that we were out of cash and that there was no choice but to shut the doors. I surprised him (and myself) by responding that the first step was for him to resign, that I would be in charge, and that I would find a way to keep the wholesale portion of the business going. I was determined to revive the business and not to "shut the doors."

The first step, unfortunately, was to reduce our staff. We had grown from twelve to twenty-four employees as a result of the Internet expansion. When the Internet funding was cut off we let go of twelve people in one day. Though I met with each person individually as well as in small groups and explained why we had to take this step, it was an extremely painful day. People were sad; some were in a state of shock; some felt betrayed; and some completely understood and appreciated how the situation was being handled.

Despite my best efforts, a few months later, the business was completely out of money. We were late paying rent, our sales reps, and our artists. The money coming in was far below our cash needs. A notable day during this time was informing the employees who had remained that we could not guarantee that we would have the money to pay the next payroll. Instead of walking away, as I feared, several employees approached me to say they had saved some money and would be interested in loaning or investing it with the company. I was touched by their loyalty and support. (They had no idea that we needed $400,000 in cash as well as steep support and commitments from vendors and investors in order to keep the doors open.)

The liabilities appeared insurmountable — the company had amassed millions of dollars in promissory notes from the Internet business, a million-dollar, five-year lease from our past office and warehouse space, and a huge severance package owed to the former CEO. This was in addition to not having the money to pay employees, reps, or bills from vendors that had accumulated.

I began working simultaneously on two fronts. First I began meeting with our suppliers, investors, landlord, and others whom we owed money to, explaining our situation. I let them know that if they each required immediate payment, we would not be able to proceed. I let them know that we intended to pay them but that we needed time. Second, I began meeting with the key prospective investors who had already invested significant funds in the Internet portion of the business to see if they would provide the needed funds not just for the business to survive but for it to thrive. My hope, of course, was that they would say yes. Instead they said they would consider investing funds but that I needed to raise a substantial portion of total funds needed from other sources before they would make their investments.

This was quite discouraging since I had no idea where else to look for investment funds. Time was running out. The key employee who had remained during these difficult months was my president, who was also my product-development person. She had attended the meeting with my investors and had hoped that our money problems would be solved. She was very upset and said that if something didn't change quickly she would leave within the next few days. Without her it would be quite difficult for me to keep the business going. And, if she left, I knew the investors would pull out and the business would most likely be forced to close.

The next morning, our president informed me that she was resigning. She could no longer stay in a situation without money and with little hope of change. I asked her not to resign and suggested that she go home for three days and not think about Brush Dance. I told her that I needed this time to raise the money or at least to prove that I could raise the money. If I hadn't accomplished this in three days, she should resign.

She went home. I sat at my desk, cried for a few minutes, then got to work. I made a list of everyone I could think of calling who either might be able to invest in Brush Dance or who might know of someone who could invest. Then I began calling everyone on the list. Most people said no. A few said yes. Some people said maybe or pledged their help in assisting me in raising the funds.

Three days later I hadn't quite reached the needed goal, but I was close. I sent an email to the key investors telling them just where things stood in relation to raising my share of the needed funds. I also told them that I needed their commitment by the next morning or I would shut down the company.

When I arrived at work at 6:00 the next morning, I found an email from the investors saying, "Congratulations. We will transfer our portion of the funds today." My president returned to work since we had the funds the team needed to move the business forward. Now we could get back to the day-to-day business of working to reach financial stability.

I've learned more than I care to from mistakes, from "bad" decisions, and from failure. I take some (but not much) solace in the description of a Zen teacher's life as being "one continuous mistake," and at the same time I see the immense wisdom in this statement. As long as we are always trying, always aiming high, there will be constant failure, constant falling short of what we set out to accomplish. As the twelfth-century Christian mystic Teresa of Avila said, "I know the Universe won't give me anything I can't handle. I just wish it didn't trust me so much."

QUESTIONS FOR DAILY PRACTICE

- What are some of your failures in business or at work?

- What lessons have you learned from these failures?

- What is your definition of failure? What is your definition of success?

- What are some of your successes at work?

- What have you learned from these successes?

- If you could be assured of not failing, what might you attempt?

TENACITY

Growing up I always believed that my family was wealthy. Though I didn't want much as a child, it always seemed like I got most of the things I wanted. When I was a junior in high school I was accepted to early admissions at Rutgers University. I was excited to inform my parents, who were very happy for me. Then my mother looked at me and asked how I was planning to pay for it. She informed me that our family did not have any money to contribute to my college education. This came as quite a shock.

The next day I went to my high school counselor and asked for some ideas about how to pay for college. She handed me a thick book listing scholarships. I spent hours scouring the book, looking for some kind of scholarship that I might be eligible for. I was a good student and a good athlete, but not outstanding at anything. Then I came across a listing for a golf caddie scholarship — an ex-caddie had left an endowment for caddies to go to college. I looked up the codes and found that Rutgers and the golf course where I had caddied during previous summers were eligible for this scholarship. I went to the golf professional at the local course, who told me to write a letter of recommendation and he would sign it. A few months later I received a letter of congratulations saying that I was to be given a caddie scholarship and a work study position that would pay for my tuition and housing in full. Although I wasn't particularly conscious of it at the time, this was an incident where tenacity had a major effect on my life.

Several years ago I read an *Inc.* magazine study about factors separating businesses that succeed from those that fail. The primary predictor that a business will survive is that the owner or management team has no choice but to make the business work. This generally means the person or people who own the business are dependent on it for their income. It means that if the business were to fail, the owners would have substantial personal financial liability. It also means that there is a commitment beyond money, having to do with values or identity. When management believes there is no choice but to make the business work, the chance of success is greatly increased.

Though I have experienced my share of difficulties, challenges, and pain during these past fifteen years of growing Brush Dance, I have also experienced a tremendous amount of satisfaction and growth. I believe firmly and completely in the product that the company creates and its potential to change lives and open hearts. I'm convinced that it is possible to develop a financially successful, spiritually based company. I love the complexity, simplicity, and mystery of how this business works. I love the challenges of combining flexibility, creativity, and discipline. I am willing to tenaciously battle and overcome whatever obstacles I may face. If change is needed, so be it. If the company needs to be reinvented, okay, change and transformation seem to come with the territory. If I need to stretch myself beyond my perceived patterns and limitations (gulp), then okay.

I recently turned on the radio and heard the conductor for the New York Philharmonic Orchestra being interviewed. He talked about his family being killed in Nazi Germany and being raised by an aunt in Europe. When he was nine years old he didn't speak for an entire year. At the end of the year he heard someone playing the piano, the first time he had ever heard the instrument. He immediately knew that he wanted to play the piano and began taking lessons.

The interviewer asked him if he had a natural talent as a child for the piano, since he is now regarded as one of the world's greatest pianists. He was silent for several moments in response to this question. He then said that the question didn't really register with him. It was irrelevant whether or not he had talent for the piano. When he heard the piano, he was possessed — he had to play.

The other day I relayed to my purchasing manager the phrase that described how I wanted her to perform in her role: "compassionate bulldog." When getting pricing from vendors and when sourcing for new products, it is important to be tenacious, to not take no for an answer, to always be digging deeper for more information, more options, and better pricing. When you run into obstacles, you need to keep going, to find new solutions, to find better prices and better ways of doing things. At the same time, it is important to take good care of people in the process. In fact, getting answers and getting good prices depend on forming good relationships with people, not by putting them off or being confrontational.

It is sometimes said that success is one-tenth inspiration and nine-tenths perspiration. Dogen, in talking about the quest for awakening, says that it is necessary to fail ninety-nine times before we can have one glimpse of our true nature.

QUESTIONS FOR DAILY PRACTICE

- When have you overcome immense obstacles?

- What did you learn from these experiences?

- When have you given up?

- When have you acted with compassion in difficult situations, and when have you not?

- When are you a compassionate bulldog at work?

LET CASH BE YOUR KING,
BUT LET FLEXIBILITY BE YOUR GOD

When I was in charge of the draft horse farming project at Green Gulch, my duties included taking care of the horses as well as our Jersey milk cow, Daisy. One morning, in the midst of my morning work period, Daisy became ill. I found her lying on her side in her stall. I knew that if she stayed in this position for long she would die. I was able to coax her to sit up, but to keep her sitting up I had to lean my back against the side of the shed and hold her up by putting my feet just below her neck and use my body as a kind of lever. I was able to get someone's attention so that she could call the veterinarian. Several hours later the veterinarian arrived, injected Daisy with a drug, and she popped back up onto her feet.

I didn't pop up quite as quickly. I was sore and exhausted. As I was walking toward my room, someone came running over to me yelling that Snip, one of our draft horses, was stuck in the mud. I had no idea what this meant but knew that I had to go investigate. Snip was in the back pasture, which contained a large pond. She had been drinking from the pond and had sunken into the mud up to the tops of her legs. And she appeared to be slowly sinking further. We tried calling her and then, with the help of several more people, tied some ropes around her and pulled. Finally, as it was growing dark, we called the local fire department. When they arrived they wrapped fire hoses around Snip's torso. By this time nearly all fifty Green Gulch residents had come out to watch the spectacle. This was a good thing, since we needed everyone's help. We asked everyone to pull on the hoses and in this way were able to slowly extract Snip from the mud.

Working as a Zen farmer taught me a tremendous amount about flexibility, which has served me well in my role as CEO of a growing publishing company. Every day, working with the horses and cows, was unpredictable. Each day began with a plan and a list of things to accomplish. Then life on the farm unfolded.

Every day at work is unique and unpredictable. Employees call in sick or resign. The phone rings and a customer orders a large amount of a product that we don't have in stock. An important order does not reach our customer on time. An artist has a family emergency and is unable to create a design that we promised to a customer. Specialty retail stores, our primary customer base, begin to struggle, and each year more and more of our customers go out of business. Every few years our computer systems become outdated. As we grow, our software becomes outdated, and at some point useless.

Flexibility means responding to whatever is needed. It usually requires responding to change and simultaneously not losing sight of the big picture. At times the situation requires that we alter the so-called big picture by changing the business model or by changing direction dramatically.

After flexibility, cash is the second most important resource in business. It is the lifeblood of the daily operation of business. Ultimately, for any business to be viable, more cash must come in than goes out. It is just that simple. A business mentor of mine says that the cardinal rules about cash in business are: 1) if your business is doing well, you need more cash — to fund growth — and 2) if your business is doing badly, you need more cash — to fund your losses. In any case, you always need more cash.

Flexibility has taken on god status because it allows you to meet and respond to change. Everything in business is in constant flux — you, your staff, technology, and the needs of your customers, competitors, and the business environment. Flexibility allows you to make adjustments to your business as necessary, and if need be, to alter your business model to meet changing circumstances.

Flexibility also enables you to see that there are many ways to bring cash in and many ways to reduce cash flow out. Cash flow can be increased by borrowing, by selling stock, by having customers pay sooner. Cash flow can be increased by adding sales volume. Cash out can be decreased by negotiating better terms with vendors, by cutting expenses, by reducing inventory, or by scaling down operations. Flexibility allows you to adjust not only to cash needs but also to changes in the environment, to personnel issues, and to the vast number of factors and variables in the life of any business.

Zen and business share the same ultimate goal: flexibility and responsiveness. Zen practice helps us to develop a flexible, responsive mind, free of assumptions and habits, free of ruts and patterns. Businesses exist to meet the changing needs of customers. Understanding and meeting these needs require flexibility and responsiveness.

QUESTIONS FOR DAILY PRACTICE

- What is your relationship with money?
- How does making money rate on your list of priorities?

- How flexible are you when it comes to money?

- How are you flexible at work? What are the key elements of this flexibility?

- How are you inflexible at work? What are the key elements of this inflexibility?

YOU CAN CHANGE

THE WORLD

BE MINDFUL OF THE NEEDS YOU MEET

I had a teacher in business school who was fierce, intimidating, and a sweetheart. Ian McMillan was a wiry South African with a quick wit and a quick temper. He taught a class entitled "Entrepreneurship." Our weekly assignment was to find and describe a business opportunity that came from our own experience. We had to spot a need that could be met by forming a business. In one page we were to describe the need, how our business idea would meet this need, and the general business proposition.

I think we all received Cs or Ds on the first weeks' assignments. Professor McMillan handed them back and said they were complete trash. He said we weren't really looking for needs, for real problems, and that our business ideas stank. He announced that we needed to be obsessed with seeking out needs and with finding solutions and that we needed to offer proof that our idea had the potential to become a viable business. Week after week this assignment continued. By the fourth and fifth weeks of the semester there were a few Bs, and by the twelfth week the grades were primarily As and Bs.

Having this assignment each week forced me to look everywhere for needs. I was indeed obsessed, looking at the world in a different way. Wherever I was — while riding on the subway, in my home, or taking the elevator to class — I was always looking at what was needed and thinking about how these needs could be met through a business. I began to see needs everywhere. On the subway there was a need for better maps of the subway system, a need for a place to store wet umbrellas, a need for a system of letting people on and off the trains. While caring for my infant son I thought about the need for more information about child rearing, about better car seats, and things that were needed to help him get a good night's sleep.

I started Brush Dance with the intention of meeting people's need to help the environment by using recycled paper products. At that time it was nearly impossible to find products made from recycled materials. It soon became apparent that we were inadvertently meeting another need — the need for sending cards that combined meaningful words and unique artwork. No one was making cards that had quotes on the front, and few cards had much depth.

I am constantly evaluating what needs our business meets and experimenting with a variety of business models. As the retail market becomes more and more difficult to penetrate, Brush Dance has begun exploring partnering with schools and nonprofits looking for ways to raise funds. We make products that appear to fit this need. Brush Dance is also looking into selling our products directly to individuals through an Internet site. While we stay focused on our central business of selling to stores, it is essential that we explore alternatives.

Businesses exist to meet the needs of people. The larger and more complex and technologically driven business becomes, the easier it is to lose sight of this simple truth. This truth seems so old-fashioned in our complex society, but if we look closely, the model remains the same — business provides goods and services to meet the needs of people.

QUESTIONS FOR DAILY PRACTICE

- What needs does your work or business meet?

- How are these needs changing?

- What needs do you see as unfulfilled in your work environment?

- What needs do you see in your life as unfulfilled? How could business meet those needs?

RADICAL LISTENING

The day after Brush Dance changed course, from pursuing an Internet strategy to returning to our core wholesale business, I called an emergency staff meeting. I expressed my appreciation of our remaining staff as well as my concern for how much stress everyone must be feeling, given the recent changes. Our controller, who is usually quite reserved, blurted out, "We are not feeling worried or anxious. We are relieved. If you don't believe me, ask everyone!" I turned to the person sitting to my left and said, "Dwayne, what are you feeling? How do you feel about what just happened and where we are now?" Dwayne spoke from his heart. Everyone listened, giving him the space to speak his truth. There was no commenting, no questions, no responding. We went around the room so that each person could speak. This simple act of listening and of feeling heard was very powerful. Most everyone was relieved that the company had refocused its strategy and pared down in size. Everyone could see that the dot-com approach was not working and was relieved to be focused again on our core wholesale business.

When I teach my spirituality and business retreats, I am often surprised by the number of people who feel that they cannot speak openly and honestly at work. People believe that their feelings and ideas are not welcome. This is perhaps the most common and pervasive experience in the business community. In these workshops we generally spend time in groups of three or four people. Each person in the group takes a turn, speaking for six or seven minutes. During this time we ask that other members of the group just listen, without asking questions or making suggestions. Just speaking and having others listen can be a powerful and unusual experience. Just listening and not thinking about what to say next can be equally as powerful.

The practice of meditation, the heart of Zen practice, is the practice of radical listening. While sitting still we practice listening to our bodies. We allow our awareness to sweep from the top of our heads down to the tips of our toes, touching every part of our body on the way. We check in with how our body feels and notice where we are holding tension and where we are loose. We listen carefully and closely to our breathing, following our breath all the way in and all the way out. We feel our breath as it touches our nostrils as we breathe in and again as we exhale. We notice how our breath fills our lungs and then affects all the parts of our body. We listen to our thoughts and to the spaces in between our thoughts. We listen to our surroundings, to the sounds of others in the room, to the birds, to the garbage trucks.

At work, we take what we learn from this listening practice and notice that while working, while speaking, while talking on the phone, while driving, we have the opportunity to notice our bodies and our breathing. At the same time we listen to others and to the sounds around us. We learn to focus and just to be with whatever we are doing. And, just as in our meditation practice, when we are distracted, we come back by returning to our bodies and our breathing.

Listen to the sounds in your office, the voices, the hum of computers, the sounds from outside. Just stop and listen.

When in conversation, listen fully. If your own ideas or responses start to form, watch them come and go; then return your attention to the person speaking. When the person stops, wait; allow a space before responding. Acknowledge that you've heard and understood what was said. Listen to yourself fully — listen to your heart beating. Listen to the sound of your breath. Yes, we all breathe at work!

QUESTIONS FOR DAILY PRACTICE

- In what kinds of situations do you find it easy to listen fully?

- What makes it difficult for you to listen fully?

- What gets in the way of your being present?

APPRECIATING UNCERTAINTY

Last summer my twenty-year-old son, Jason, worked in the Brush Dance warehouse. I received the benefit of his insights about the company as well as his suggestions for improvements. Fairly often Jason would suggest that I take him to lunch, and though this meant spending more money than I normally would, the opportunity made me happy.

During one of our many lunch discussions he asked me, "Do you think of yourself as a confident person?" This was the day before I was scheduled to give a lecture at Green Gulch Farm. He went on to say that he was trying to understand how I could be giving lectures, teaching, and running a company. He saw me as somewhat quiet and shy and had a difficult time seeing me as a teacher. "After all, you've never taught me anything," he blurted out. After my initial surprise at hearing these words, I teased him by responding that I had been planning a lecture series for him, which was scheduled to begin the following week.

I went on to explain that as a Zen teacher and as a businessman my confidence lies in the knowledge that I am certain of nothing. I have no idea where I came from or where I am going. I have no idea what will happen to Brush Dance in the future. Realizing and facing this directly, how do we find our own calm, flexibility, and freedom? I think that this is the kind of confidence that Zen students and businesspeople are constantly cultivating — tremendous confidence and trust in our own sincerity and in our effort and in our ability to meet whatever comes our way, the confidence in our ability not to get in the way of our deepest intentions.

On a practical level, we need to have confidence and some trust or faith in ourselves and in our abilities. Ideally, just enough to continually try things that may be beyond our comfort level. Again, in another paradox, cultivating a sense of confidence, a sense of certainty, allows us to jump into the unknown.

Often when I see friends or family whom I have not seen for a while, people will ask me how Brush Dance is doing. I find this a difficult question to answer. Wanting to give a truthful answer, I usually say that we are either on the verge of tremendous success, or we are on the verge of tremendous failure. We have the potential for success in that we make great products, many with the potential to become wildly popular. Our card line or journals could suddenly take off. Perhaps Oprah will discover us and mention our cards or calendars on her show. Or perhaps one of our new product ideas will be picked up by major chains throughout the country.

Brush Dance also has the potential to fail. We have few cash reserves and very few key managers, making complete failure very easy to imagine. We could lose a few key customers or a key employee, or customers could stop buying our products. Each day Brush Dance is dependent on the number of orders that come through our fax machine. We are much like a store, not knowing how many people will come in and how many will purchase something. All businesses, in this very basic way, live with tremendous uncertainty. Private schools don't know how many students will enroll each semester; therapists don't know how many clients will stay or leave; businesses never know when customers will stop using their products or services.

There is a Zen story in which the Zen master becomes ill. He had always been a healthy and vigorous teacher. One of the monks asks him, "Are you well or not?" The teacher responds by saying, "Sun-faced Buddha, Moon-faced Buddha." The Sun-faced Buddha is supposed to live for more than a thousand years. The Moon-faced Buddha lives only one day and one night. The point of the story is that none of us knows what the future brings. All we can do is be composed, be ourselves, and meet our lives fully. We never know whether we have one day to live or a thousand years. In any case, all we can do is be open and present and make our best effort.

QUESTIONS FOR DAILY PRACTICE

- What are you certain of in your work?

- What are you not certain of in your work?

- How do you feel about uncertainty? How do your feelings about uncertainty help you? How do they hinder you?

SIT-DOWN COMEDY: HUMOR AT WORK

Be here now. Be someplace else later.
Is that so complicated?
— David Bader

I've recently begun thinking that my next career may be to
become a "sit-down" comedian. Whereas stand-up comedy is
aimed at being funny and making people laugh, sit-down comedy
would be aimed at being funny and helping people to awaken, to
free themselves of false views, and to be more appreciative and
alive. The main thrust of sit-down comedy would be allowing
people to see that what we think of as a solid, substantial self, with
all its associated problems and concerns, is a fiction. Once we realize this, we have just enough distance from our thoughts, assumptions, and problems that we can laugh at ourselves. Since we are all
born and we will all die, what isn't funny? Sit-down comedy would,
of course, be performed sitting down.

Humor in Zen? Humor at work? Maybe you are shaking your
head in disbelief. I'm not talking about Zen jokes. I think there are
only two, which you probably know: What did the Zen student say
to the hot dog vendor? Make me one with everything. Why can't
Zen students vacuum under furniture? No attachments.

Zen doesn't need jokes to be funny. The joke is that *everything*
is the joke. Some people might think that Zen does not have much
of a developed written or oral tradition when it comes to humor,

211

but actually when you look closely, Zen is filled with playfulness and trickery. There is a famous Zen story in the form of a question and answer: The student asks, "What is Buddha?" The teacher answers, "The oak tree in the courtyard." This is pretty funny stuff! I began a recent lecture at the San Francisco Zen Center with a joke: What's the difference between stand-up comedy and a Zen lecture? Stand-up comedy isn't always funny.

After one of my recent lectures in San Francisco, a man asked me why Zen lectures tend to be humorous. I answered that once you have been sitting meditation, facing a wall, morning after morning, year after year, everything begins to appear funny. Zen teaching starts from the premise that there is no avoiding suffering and that thinking that a self exists, separate from others, is the basic cause of all pain and suffering — again, pretty funny stuff!

From the perspective of Zen practice, everything in business, everything at work, is funny. Human beings are strange, unexplainable, hilarious creatures. Just notice how people look, what they say, what their intentions are. Notice the gaps; notice that interactions and feelings are unpredictable and messy. We are all beginners, all amateurs at being human, at interacting with others.

Work is a great playground, a grand theater for humans to express themselves and to interact with each other and with the material world and spiritual world. Misunderstandings, unsolvable problems, emotional outbursts, broken plans and impossible strategies, posturing, endless meetings, unexpected successes, terrible failures — all funny. People fall in love at work, or they learn to hate each other. (I've noticed recently at Brush Dance that this seems to be the case with our employees; there's very little middle ground between love and hate.) People discover hidden talents or hidden anger, rise to meet new challenges, or discover blind spots that had not been fully disclosed.

I was recently surprised to learn that Brush Dance had been receiving many orders as a result of people learning about us on a local radio station. At a staff meeting my warehouse team announced that they had been sending products that had been returned and were damaged to this radio station. They listen to this station each day at work and really enjoy that the radio personalities mention checking out the cool products at Brush Dance. It was startling and humorous to see that our warehouse had become a success story as part of the company's marketing efforts.

Having a sense of humor may be one of the most important requirements for integrating Zen practice and work practice. The real aim of Zen practice is to be happy and to make others happy. The real purpose of business is to be happy and to make others happy.

Pay attention to the humorous aspects of your work environment.

Take the time to see what is funny at work. Let yourself smile or laugh. You can always cry later.

Experiment with responding to others in a way that is lighthearted.

QUESTIONS FOR DAILY PRACTICE

- What situations at work make you laugh, in a positive way?

- What prevents you from seeing the humorous aspects of your work?

- How can you bring more humor into your work, and into your life?

EMBRACING OUR STORIES

Several times a day, in my role as CEO of Brush Dance, I feel like the captain of a ship, at the helm, steering and guiding us with intensity through tumultuous and dangerous waters. Our sales have been down for the past three months. My management team has expressed disappointment and frustration. I hear rumblings of a kind of mutiny; some are concerned that the company is not being led in the right direction. Looming on the horizon are cash-flow shortages, and, at the same time, our busiest and most demanding season, when truckloads of calendars and holiday cards are about to be received and shipped, is fewer than thirty days away. I'm negotiating license agreements with artists and working to secure a line of credit. We are understaffed, and everyone feels stretched, and we don't have the cash to hire additional people right now.

Feeling the tensions around me and seeing some large waves and rocks up ahead, I called everyone in the company together for a meeting. I reviewed the company's mission, goals, and operating principles. I spoke openly about the problems and challenges and described the plan for meeting those challenges. I asked for everyone's support, willingness to work hard, and commitment to speak openly about their doubts and ideas. I announced that we would be implementing performance reviews, beginning with me — I would send out a 360-degree review form in which everyone in the company could review my performance. I said I would announce the results and use this information in setting my goals for the next six months. Each person in the company would then go through a similar process of review and goal setting. I felt a sense of relief and excitement after this meeting.

From a certain perspective, our work lives are much like a heroic adventure, filled with twists and turns, successes and failures, small lessons and major breakthroughs. Though Zen practice encourages us to not be caught up in or attached to our stories, it also teaches us to be intimate with and to fully embrace our stories, using them and learning from them. Seeing and understanding our stories enables us to understand the deepest and most intimate patterns, themes, and habits of our lives. Our work lives, when we pay attention, provide an amazing ground for playing out and embracing our stories.

There is a famous Chinese story about a beautiful girl named Chien, who as a child played with her cousin Chau. One day Chien's father, Kien, jestingly said to his nephew, Chau, "Some day you will marry my little daughter." Both children remembered these words and believed they would be married.

When Chien grew up, a wealthy man asked to marry her, and her father consented. Chien was very troubled by this decision but could not go against the will of her father. Chau was so angered and grieved that he decided to leave home and go to another province. He left in the night without telling anyone. Later that night he was startled when he heard the voice of Chien and saw her running along the banks of the river toward his boat. The lovers were united, found a home, had two children, and lived happily for six years.

But Chien could not stop thinking about the pain she must have caused her father and wanted to return to make amends.

Chau and Chien and their children returned to where Chien's father, Kien, lived. According to custom they decided that Chau would first go to the father's house, leaving Chien in the boat. Kien welcomed his nephew and said how worried he had been since his disappearance. Chau went on to beg Kien for his forgiveness, but Kien didn't seem to understand. Chau explained that he feared that Kien was angry for Chau's having run away with his daughter.

"What are you talking about?" said Kien. "My daughter, Chien, has been sick in bed ever since the day you disappeared."

"You daughter has not been sick," replied Chau. "She has been my wife for six years, and we have two children. We have returned to ask your forgiveness."

For a moment the two looked at each other with suspicion and amazement. Then Kien led his nephew to his daughter's room, where Chau, in amazement, saw Chien, in bed, looking sick and frail.

"Now come to the river," Chau said to the father, "for I can assure you that your daughter, despite what I saw, is in my boat."

They went to the river, and there was the daughter. Seeing her father, she bowed and wept.

Kien said to her, "If you are my daughter, I have nothing but love for you. Yet I cannot understand. Please come to my house."

As the three proceeded to the house, the sick girl, who had not left her bed for years, approached them. The two Chiens approached each other and suddenly melted into each other and became one body, one person, even more beautiful than before.

This story is a metaphor for the pain we create when our spirits and lives are not operating as one. So often people disregard their deepest passions and longings for the sake of "making a living." I've often heard this dilemma of corporate life described as "leaving your soul in the parking lot."

A Zen expression says, "Though it is the Earth that causes you to stumble and fall, it is the same Earth that you rely on to stand up." Our stories are much like this. We suffer and make mistakes because of our stories, and at the same time it is our stories that supply the important lessons in our work and lives.

Every business has a juicy story to tell, or maybe hundreds or thousands of juicy stories. It's much like looking under the hood of a car. We usually just see the outside of a car and forget about what it really is, the intricate coordination of thousands of parts, all working together. When we look "under the hood" of a business we might be surprised at what we find, at numerous levels — historical, financial, and particularly in terms of people's visions, relationships, decisions, beliefs, actions, shortcomings, and strengths. Every business and every businessperson is an amazing mass of rich, and often contradictory, mysterious stories.

Telling, hearing, and appreciating our stories of who we are and what we do at work can be a valuable vehicle for integrating our practice lives and our work lives. Completely embracing and owning our stories and at the same time seeing our stories as just that — stories — is a paradoxical and rich terrain to explore. Each of us is a hero in our own story, which began long before we were born and which will continue long after we have died.

QUESTIONS FOR DAILY PRACTICE

- How did you come to do the work you do?

- What are some stories about the work your parents did?

- What has been your greatest success at work?

- What is the story of your greatest failure at work?

WOO HOO, I FEEL REALLY DUMB

And the day came when the risk to remain in the bud
became more painful than the risk it took to blossom.
— Anaïs Nin

I learned a practice the first day of an improvisation acting class I recently took in San Francisco that changed my life and that I find applicable to the integration of Zen practice and our work lives. I'd like to teach it to you now, and I suggest that you practice it regularly. It goes like this: throw your arms high in the air over your head and let out a loud "*Woo hoo*, I feel really dumb" or "*Woo hoo*, I messed up!" Okay, one more time: "*WOO HOO*, I FEEL REALLY DUMB!" I understand that you might find this ridiculous and undignified, but just try it. Most of us could do this throughout the day, when we say something stupid, when we drop a cup, when we forget to respond to a letter or phone call, or when we notice we are acting in a way that is less than spacious or generous.

Instead of tightening our faces or hiding or feeling bad, what if we faced our mistakes directly and celebrated them? What if we created a world where we don't fear making mistakes or looking bad, a world where we can try anything? In improv and in our lives, in Zen practice and at our jobs, this is how we learn, how we develop, and how we stretch ourselves.

I've learned that the rules and assumptions of improv look a lot like Zen practice. When you are on stage you try not to do anything;

you just try to notice others and see what is needed. You don't try to say something clever or funny. You only speak when there is a need to say or do something that makes it easy for someone else to respond to — it's called making them an offer. In other words, your role is to do something that is responsive to the situation and that makes it easy for someone else to respond. In improv you are trained to accept all offers. Whatever comes your way, just accept it. Even if you don't want it or like it, just accept it. You can then use the offer or transform it in any way you want.

I also learned how much improv relies on a radical kind of mindfulness practice. If I were to ask you to act out your morning routine of getting out of bed and brushing your teeth, you would probably find, as I did, that it is very difficult to mimic each movement. To act out this routine, you have to become really aware of each movement — just as we do when we are in the meditation hall — bow to the cushion, turn clockwise, and bow away from the cushion. We have many routines like this throughout our lives, but we are generally too busy to notice them.

At the heart of Zen practice and business practice is risk taking — moving toward the unknown, moving toward what is uncomfortable. In Zen practice we do this in our meditation practice with every breath. Each time we exhale, we let go completely, not knowing for sure if there will be another breath. In this way every inhale and every exhale is precious and unknown. We recognize that we are always living on the edge of life and death. We breathe out completely, not knowing what will happen next, without any expectation.

The Buddha epitomizes the entrepreneurial spirit. Daring to reach beyond all accepted beliefs regarding the spiritual practices of his time, the Buddha delved into uncharted territory and went on to create a series of practices the world had not encountered and that have remained relevant for more than twenty-five hundred years. The Buddha first spent many years researching and experiencing the spiritual practices that were available, looked deeply at what was needed, and forged ahead with tremendous perseverance and creativity.

I generally advise all Zen students to see themselves as entrepreneurs (and all entrepreneurs to see themselves as Zen students). After all, a central teaching of the Buddha is not to accept anything that he said or taught before testing it against your own experience, your own life. This is the primary attitude of an entrepreneur. This concept — not taking anything for granted, testing assumptions, completely trusting your own experience — may appear simple and ordinary, but it is actually quite radical.

I recently gave a talk before about two hundred people at the San Francisco Zen Center. Afterward a young man approached me and said that he was sitting right up front during the lecture and noticed that my hands were shaking as I spoke, yet I seemed calm and relaxed. I told him that I noticed my hands shaking, I noticed that I was terrified, and at the same time I felt completely at home and connected to the people in the room. As I told him this I realized that this also describes how I feel most days as CEO of Brush Dance — I often feel terrified from feeling responsible for employees, artists, and customers; I feel as if I'm walking along the edge of a steep mountain, knowing that it is possible to fall, and I try to stay focused on being present, on meeting whatever arises, on giving my full energy.

The real risk in business is the same as the risk in Zen practice: to be completely yourself; to move beyond ideas of success and failure; to act with complete determination and decisiveness; to live with complete openness, flexibility, and humility; to vow and act in a way that does good and avoids harm; to not get caught by your own desires; and to be present for whatever might happen next.

QUESTIONS FOR DAILY PRACTICE

- What are your fears at work, and how do you handle these fears?

- Do you move toward your fear or away from it?

- In what ways does fear help or hinder you at work?

- What helps you feel safe enough to take risks?

- When have you been glad that you took risks? When have you wished you hadn't taken risks?

NOT YOU, NOT YOUR PROBLEMS

Two monks were arguing about the temple flag waving in the wind. One said that the flag moves. The other said that the wind moves. They argued back and forth but could not agree. Their teacher said, "Gentlemen! It is not the wind that moves; it is not the flag that moves; it is your mind that moves." The two monks were struck with awe.

This is a classic Zen story. Just when you think you might understand it, the commentary to the story goes on to say that wind, flag, and mind move: it is all the same fallacy!

In my business life I find that I often am trying to identify where the real problem lies. Is it in the current business model I have chosen? Is there a need for changes in personnel? Do I need to look more closely at myself — my patterns, my communication style, my thinking? What is the real issue? Where should I focus my attention to make Brush Dance more successful, to feel more complete and more satisfied? Is the real problem "out there" in the world or is it right here, within me? I can hear the voice of the Zen teacher from the story about the flag commenting, "Not your patterns, not your thinking, not your personnel, not the situation; not outside; not inside."

Zen practice teaches us to include everything, to have a wide view, a wide mind. Suzuki Roshi says that the purpose of Zen practice is to have a well-oriented mind and that the way to have a well-oriented mind is to realize that you are the "boss of everything." When our thoughts control us, when our problems control us, when we are driven by our feelings and emotions and ideas, they become the boss of us.

Being the "boss of everything" doesn't mean we are in control in the usual use of the word *boss*. Rather, we become completely comfortable with being fully engaged and connected to whatever we are doing. We are simultaneously letting things be, just as they are, and responding to whatever we find needs our attention.

Real composure and real effectiveness at work come from being completely responsible and taking full ownership of everything you do. At the same time your heart is open and responsive. You are not easily knocked off center or fooled by your habits or narrow ideas. You are clear about your purpose, and at the same time you are not grasping for results.

QUESTIONS FOR DAILY PRACTICE

- In what way are your strengths also your weaknesses?

- In what way are your weaknesses also your strengths?

- What throws you off center?

- What do you do to return to your center?

YOU CAN CHANGE THE WORLD

Several years ago a young woman approached me at a trade show in New York City. She wanted me to know that she had purchased a Brush Dance journal when her mother was dying. The words and artwork in this journal had a profound impact on her life and helped her during this difficult time. She said that she wanted to meet and thank me.

This was a powerful experience for me. At the time I was tired from traveling across the country and from having spent the previous day setting up our display. I was missing my family and feeling disgruntled about working on a warm spring day inside a large, stuffy building without windows. This young woman's story put my business life back in perspective. Our lives at work can have a tremendous impact on others. One smile, one act of compassion, one kind word, one real meeting of hearts can reverberate far beyond our immediate experience.

Business has a major impact on our world. Technology and the exchange of goods and services affect nearly every aspect of our daily lives. Almost every work situation and every business operates simultaneously on several levels:

Personal. We interact and engage with people daily. We touch and affect every person we contact. We can listen to people on the phone, take time to hear their pain and their stories and to share our open heart, all while conducting business. Touching the lives of people we connect with, one act of listening, of generosity, allows others to affect those people they connect with. One word, one smile really can change the world.

Community. This may include the ways in which our work influences our environment, our communities, and the towns and cities wherever we operate. Brush Dance works with many small businesses in our neighboring towns. We support a variety of fund-raising programs, supplying products to schools and non-profits that can be used to raise funds. We regularly connect with local restaurants, the post office, our forklift mechanic, and a host of other local groups and businesses. How we conduct ourselves and our business has an immediate effect on our communities.

Global. More and more businesses have a global reach, from having a presence on the Internet, to using next-day delivery, to providing the material things in our everyday and business lives. We often use, buy, or trade goods with companies from around the world. We speak to, email, and send faxes easily and regularly to people everywhere on the planet.

Brush Dance has recently begun purchasing cards and handbags from Zimbabwe, Africa. We have connected with a group of single mothers of disabled children who are selling these items to support themselves. These women are making cards by painting images on flattened bottle caps. We are now taking orders from bookstores and card shops throughout the United States for these bottle caps. We have the potential to make a substantial impact on this community in Africa.

Spiritual ideas are also transforming our world and the way we work. In the United States more than 20 million people now practice yoga. It is estimated that in the United States there are more than 50 million "cultural creatives," individuals who are values driven and have strong spiritual and environmental concerns. Prime-time television commercials feature people sitting meditation. His Holiness the Dalai Lama was featured on the cover of *Time* magazine. Spiritual thinking and concepts are slowly infiltrating all aspects of our culture and the world culture. As individuals and as businesses, by integrating spiritual values with our work we are on the forefront of bringing about a major transformation of values.

I often go into work early on Sunday mornings. It is usually very quiet, since I'm often the only person in the building. It is a time for me to think about and plan for the upcoming week and to examine some longer-term strategies. One Sunday morning I got up from my desk and went into my warehouse to find a greeting card to send to a prospective customer. I opened the door to the warehouse, took a deep breath, and was awestruck. I saw rows of metal racks from one end of the warehouse to the other, from the floor almost to the high ceilings, filled with boxes. Where did all these cards, journals, and calendars come from? How did an idea about starting a recycled paper business turn into this?

For that moment I felt deeply grateful to be managing a company that creates and distributes inspirational messages. Often I am so consumed by the day-to-day pressures of making payroll, working with people, and solving problems that I lose sight of the impact that business has on the world.

QUESTIONS FOR DAILY PRACTICE

- How do your actions and your work affect your colleagues, your community, and the global community?

- What practices can you use in working with these three groups?

- What negative impacts does your work have? What are the positive impacts?

IF IT'S NOT PARADOXICAL,
IT'S NOT TRUE!

*Paradox: a statement that seems contradictory, absurd,
or unbelievable but that may be true; a person, situation, or act
that seems to have contradictory or inconsistent qualities.*
— Webster's Dictionary

When I first lived at Tassajara my parents and brother came to visit me during the summer guest season. They appreciated the natural beauty of Tassajara but missed the comforts of civilization such as sidewalks and easily accessible hot running water. After a few days we left Tassajara and flew directly to Las Vegas, where my parents like to go for vacation. I was surprised at how comfortable and at home I felt there.

Though paradoxical, I noticed many similarities between life in a Zen monastery and life in a casino. Both entities were focused on greed: a monastery is focused on freeing people from greed, while a casino celebrates greed. Both places work toward transcending time. Monastery life is on a strict schedule in which individuals give themselves over to following the schedule outside their usual desires and activities. Casinos don't have clocks so that people can give themselves over to the schedule of nonstop gambling instead of following their usual routines.

Everything about us and our lives is filled with paradox. I am extremely energetic and very lazy. I see myself as successful and as far from being a success. I am very detail oriented and quite sloppy. I negotiate well for others and terribly for myself. I love to write, and I hate to write.

We can control our breathing, and our breathing is completely outside our control. We have no idea how our bodies and minds work. The fact that we find ourselves alive, in this time, in this place, in this body is completely beyond our comprehension. Nothing about our lives makes sense. Our lives are unbelievable, contradictory, and inconsistent.

Our lives, when we look at them carefully, are messy, contradictory, unexplainable, absurd, and mysterious. We fall in love, we follow our passions, our feelings change, our passions change, our partners change, our businesses change. Events take place, life happens. Our work lives are filled with contradictions and mystery — we don't know why we are doing what we do, what works and what doesn't work. What appears stuck may be the beginning of an opening, and what appears open may be stuck. What is satisfying one day may be frustrating another. A popular product turns into a dud. A successful marketing strategy is repeated and fails miserably.

Being an effective leader, manager, or worker requires that you embrace skills and attitudes that appear to be in conflict, not sticking to either side, such as:

Patient	⟷	Decisive
Beginner	⟷	Experienced
Surrender	⟷	Control
Inclusive	⟷	Focused
Humble	⟷	Confident
Open	⟷	Strong
Flexible	⟷	Tenacious

Each situation we encounter requires its own response. Different skills and approaches are required to effectively engage with whatever circumstances we find ourselves in.

This afternoon I met with one of our key artists. He was describing a very difficult problem, a way in which his family business, consisting of several art galleries, had divided into two distinctive camps regarding how to operate the business. Maneuvering through these differences while maintaining family relationships was difficult and painful. He said he was tired of fighting and had decided that it was a better course to surrender. I understood his dilemma, since it is a choice that I am regularly faced with. When he asked my advice I told him that yes, sometimes it is the right choice to surrender. At other times it may be better to surrender to the fight. Surrendering didn't necessarily mean giving in. In this case he might choose to resolve the issue not by giving in but by going after what he really wanted.

Embracing paradox is not really any different from accepting what is, accepting the truth of our situations and of our lives. Simplicity and clarity generally require not seeing the various sides and layers of our work and our lives. As the title to this chapter states: If it's not paradoxical, it's not true.

QUESTIONS FOR DAILY PRACTICE

- What is paradoxical about you?

- What is paradoxical about your work?

- How do you hold opposing and contradictory ideas?

- When is it difficult for you to hold opposing ideas?

ACT AS THOUGH YOU KNOW
WHAT YOU ARE DOING

When Brush Dance was in its infancy, I called an attorney friend whom I had met while living at Green Gulch Farm. He had become a senior partner with a prestigious law firm in San Francisco. I asked him if he could refer me to a good lawyer to help me with some Brush Dance legal issues. He responded that he thought I should work with the best lawyers in the city, and that meant working with his company. He realized that being a start-up company, we would not be able to afford his company, so he proposed assigning me to a very skilled junior attorney who would charge me far less than the company's usual rates. He would consider this an investment, hoping that as Brush Dance grew we would be able to hire his firm at their regular rates.

I began to work with Ed Power, a third-year lawyer who had graduated from Stanford Law School. I told him that I needed to raise money to grow the business. He suggested that the company do a private stock offering. He would supply me with the necessary documents and teach me how to amend them to fit the needs of Brush Dance. Since I would be doing most of the work, he would charge me very little money. A simple private offering generally costs a minimum of $10,000 to $20,000. His firm charged me

$2,000. From this experience I learned the details of putting together a private equity offering. The next time I needed to raise funds I had to work with a different lawyer, since Ed was no longer with the firm. This lawyer was shocked when I told him that I would put together the offering and just needed a small amount of advice and guidance.

So often in business I find myself doing things that I don't know how to do — directing artists, making presentations, writing business plans, developing new products, or overseeing accountants. Sometimes I'm called on to be the computer expert or the human resources expert or the legal expert or the financial expert. Without acting foolishly or hastily, by asking lots of questions and by being aware of what I really don't know, I often must act as if I know what I'm doing, forge ahead, and learn as I go. The more I do, the more I stumble along, the more I learn.

Suzuki Roshi said, "In the beginner's mind there are many possibilities, but in the expert's there are few." He was advising his students to be open, "to not lose the limitless meaning of original mind." Acting as though you know what you are doing is much like "beginner's mind" applied to our work lives. A beginner approaches each situation as new and fresh, as a situation in which to learn and to grow. A beginner is not hindered by habits and fear.

When Brush Dance first began, my garage was our warehouse, my living room was our office, and my foyer was our shipping room. In September 1989 we mailed five thousand one-page catalogs to a mailing list of individuals. We were surprised and pleased by the volume of orders that began to appear each day in our mailbox. I hired a high school student to help me ship the daily orders of wrapping paper and greeting cards.

Carlos was the company's first employee. He came each day

after school, and I gave him the written customer orders that I had processed the night before. He then pulled the products from shelves in the garage and packed the orders, sitting on the floor of our foyer. One day a friend, who ran a small business, came to visit and suggested that we get a table in our foyer for packing orders instead of packing them on the floor. This was a novel and breakthrough idea! Not having the funds to buy a table, we borrowed a door and two sawhorses from a neighbor. Brush Dance had its first shipping table. Though we may have been acting as though we knew what we were doing, we didn't have a clue! As I write this, I'm afraid there are many situations that exist today at Brush Dance, fifteen years later, that are not so different from packing orders on the floor.

Our work lives can be a great playground for discovering our "original minds." So jump in. Get started. Learn well by watching, engaging, doing. Appreciate repetition. Relish boredom. Build good habits, develop a disciplined approach. Then forge ahead. Be humble. Appreciate your mistakes. Act as though you know what you are doing.

QUESTIONS FOR DAILY PRACTICE

- What are some work situations that you entered without really knowing what you were doing? What happened? What did you learn?

- How do you usually approach work situations when you feel unsure or intimidated?

- What are you afraid of at work? What helps you to feel safe?

EPILOGUE

As the final touches are being made to this book, another chapter of my life unfolds. About two years ago at a breakfast meeting, one of my mentors, who is also a Brush Dance board member, looked me in the eyes and said, "It is time for you to leave Brush Dance. You have other things to do, much larger things." I gulped. I was shocked. Tears filled my eyes. I knew she was right, and I could also feel my fear and resistance to change.

It seems to take me a few years to realize and implement major changes in my life. Though my instincts are clear, it often takes me a while to listen and act. Though part of me was holding on to the idea of continuing to grow Brush Dance, I could also hear the voice of one of my business school professors: "The person who starts the business is *never* the right person to grow it." Though I don't completely agree with this statement, it was becoming obvious that Brush Dance needed a different style of leadership and even more obvious that it was time for me to take the leap and leave. During a meeting with my board a few months ago, we set in motion a plan to hire new leadership and for me to transition out of the company.

Today is day twelve of my not sitting in the Brush Dance CEO seat. I feel much like a parent, grieving as I watch my teenager, who I have nurtured, cared for, and become identified with, separate from me, ready to take flight. But there's glowing, too, in observing one's own teenagers and business ventures enter a new phase of maturity.

And I feel "pregnant" with the idea of starting and building a new company, much as I did fifteen years ago when I first had the thought to begin Brush Dance. I've begun creating a coaching and consulting company with the mission of "relieving suffering in the business world," and I have called the company ZBA Associates. The need is enormous and obvious. It is also clear that this was my vision when I left Tassajara to go to business school in New York City twenty years ago.

I'm sitting at my kitchen table, completing this book. As I look around my kitchen I see the pervasive impact of business, from the laptop computer in front of me, the candles on the table, the container of yogurt, the phone book, the newspaper, and the teapot, all produced by groups of people working together. Each thing has a purpose and a history. Each object helps me in some way. Each was made by a human being with an amazing story, working for a company with an amazing story.

I shake my head in disbelief that I have written a book about Zen and business. I remember Jennifer Futernick's incredulous expression, shortly after we met when I was director of Tassajara, when I told her I was thinking of applying to business school. Jennifer, a summer guest at Tassajara, was one of the editors of *In Search of Excellence,* one of the most successful business books ever written and one of the first books to connect business success with employing our values. Jennifer later also edited my business school applications. But I could see from her first expression that she felt nothing could be more radically in opposition than Zen and business. She has now read a draft of this book and says I have convinced her otherwise.

My daughter, who is now sixteen, read part of this book, put it down, and looked up at me with a serious expression. "You can do better than this, Dad. This can be a great book. These are important ideas. These ideas can change people's lives. I don't think you are trying hard enough. You are not stressed out enough." I told her that I had been writing this book for nearly ten years and that this book actually began more than twenty years ago when I was director of Tassajara. I suggested that perhaps I needed to smoke cigarettes and drink whiskey to demonstrate to her my true stress level. But I do hope, without resorting to tobacco and alcohol, that I've offered some ideas to change your life.

As I complete this process of writing, I feel much like I did when I was completing my time as head student during a three-month practice period at the San Francisco Zen Center. Each of the fifty people in the practice period and twenty others who had previously been head student asked me a question. I did my best to meet each person and answer his or her question. The ceremony ends with the head student making a statement; a variation of this statement feels appropriate to make at this time: "I have written this book with the support of countless people. I did not deserve this opportunity. If my words have misled you in any way, please wash out your ears. I will continue to practice and will try harder. Please continue your practice."

There is a statement attributed to the historical Buddha, more than twenty-five hundred years ago: "Your work is to discover your work and with all your heart give yourself to it." Work, discover, heart. May we mix all these ingredients in just the right quantities, helping ourselves and each other. May all beings be happy. May we give ourselves to our work and to the work of our lives.

NINE PRACTICES FOR BEING
MORE IN CONNECTION WITH YOURSELF
WHILE AT WORK

1. Put an "altar" on your desk, some meaningful object or words, a picture of an important place, teacher, or friend, or an inspiring quote.

2. Place an "altar" in your pocket — a stone or shell or bead, something that is meaningful or special to you and brings you back to your breath.

3. When you walk through your office doorway, slow down and notice which foot you enter the room with. Instead of walking through the center of the doorway, enter through the left or right side. If you walk through the left side, step over the threshold of the doorway with your left foot. If you walk through the right side, step over the threshold with your right foot. (These are the instructions for entering a Zen meditation hall.)

4. When the phone rings, take a deep breath. Know that the person calling you is also taking a breath.

5. Bow to your chair when you arrive and leave work. If bowing would look too strange in your office, just stop and take a breath when you arrive and leave.

6. Practice "right speech" — be open, honest, and compassionate with yourself and others. Speak the truth.

7. Realize that, as Suzuki Roshi says, "You are perfect just as you are, and you can use a little improvement."

8. Practice generosity, not by giving material things but by giving your presence, your caring, and your kindness.

9. Take fifteen minutes of quiet time every day. During this time, observe your breath and your body. Find a place to sit or walk by yourself.

THE Z.B.A. MANIFESTO

1. It's okay not to know. It's okay to be vulnerable. No one has all the answers. We value and learn from the questions and the asking.

2. We are learning to appreciate the mystery and sacredness of our lives and the mystery and sacredness of life.

3. Life is short. There is no escape from old age, sickness, and death. Death is a great teacher. Recognizing the shortness of our lives provides motivation to live fully in each day and in each moment.

4. We understand the importance of taking regular quiet time for ourselves. Through reflection and by slowing down we develop an appreciation for life and we increase our capacity for understanding.

5. We are learning to trust our inner wisdom. Our bodies and minds are amazing, unexplainable, and unfathomable.

6. It's okay to be uneasy, to be uncomfortable, to grieve, to feel pain. Recognizing when something is off, feeling the depth of loss, experiencing pain, is the first step toward change and growth.

7. Practice active listening — listening deeply to yourself and to others. Listen to others without formulating your own ideas. Listen to yourself before speaking.

8. We all seek balance in our lives — balancing work and family, balancing our inner and outer lives, balancing what we want to do and what we must do.

9. We are learning that we can be fully ourselves in all situations — at work, as parents, as children, as friends, as lovers.

10. Being ourselves at work is vital to our health and happiness. Our time is too valuable to sell, at any price.

11. Each moment is precious. In every moment we have an opportunity to discover, to grow, to speak the truth.

12. Each moment is ordinary. In every moment we can realize we are fine just as we are. Nothing else is needed.

13. We appreciate what is paradoxical. What may at first seem contradictory or beyond our understanding may be true. After all, who is it that is breathing? Who is it that dreams? How is it that these hands effortlessly glide along this keyboard?

14. Age is a state of mind. We have the opportunity to grow to be more like ourselves every day.

15. Developing intimate relationships is a vital part of our lives and our development. Intimacy requires openness, honesty, and vulnerability.

16. Real, honest, open communication is highly valued — and takes real skill and effort.

17. When we slow down and learn to trust ourse
    arises naturally.

18. When we slow down and learn to trust ourselves, creativ-
    ity arises naturally.

19. Self-knowledge and understanding require persistence
    and perseverance. Developing awareness and balance is an
    ongoing, unending process.

20. Self-knowledge and understanding require discipline.
    Whatever path we take requires structure, guidelines, and
    feedback.

21. Self-knowledge and understanding require courage.

22. Diversity is essential. Our differences enrich our lives.
    There is no "other," just as our right hand is not a stranger
    to our left hand.

23. A simple rule to follow is do good, avoid harm. Of course,
    this is not simple or easy.

24. There are many paths and many practices toward devel-
    oping awareness and personal growth.

25. Our everyday lives and activities provide fertile ground
    for developing growth and understanding.

26. We can learn to appreciate the gifts we've received from
    our parents and to forgive them. We understand on a deep
    level all we have received from the generations that have
    come before us.

27. We feel a deep responsibility for our children and for the
    generations that will come after us.

28. We can all act as change agents. We can choose to take action in improving and healing our environment and our society. There is no shortage of issues to address, of healing to take place.

29. We are all change agents on a personal level — we either create healing amongst those we live and work with or we create stress.

30. We can choose to act as change agents in relation to our communities.

31. We can choose to act as change agents in relation to our society or on a global level.

32. Everything we hold dear will one day change and disappear. Every business that now exists will one day cease. Every person now alive will one day die.

33. At a deep level, we realize that we are neither in control nor not in control. Our task is to paddle the boat, with awareness and integrity. The flow of the river is outside our doing.

34. We all have the power to find peace and happiness in the midst of change and impermanence.

35. We have the power to heal ourselves, our communities, and our planet.

RECOMMENDED READING

Aitkin, Robert. *The Gateless Barrier: The Wu-Men Kuan.* Berkeley, CA: Northpoint Press, 1991.

———. *The Practice of Perfection: The Paramitas from a Zen Buddhist Perspective.* Washington, D.C.: Counterpoint Press, 1997.

Barks, Coleman. *The Essential Rumi.* San Francisco: HarperSanFrancisco, 1997.

Batchelor, Stephen. *Buddhism Without Beliefs: A Contemporary Guide to Awakening.* New York: Riverhead Books, 1998.

Bly, Robert, ed. *Selected Poems of Rainer Maria Rilke.* New York: Harper & Row, 1981.

Chödrön, Pema. *When Things Fall Apart: Heart Advice for Difficult Times.* Boston: Shambhala, 2000.

Fischer, Norman. *Taking Our Places: The Buddhist Path to Truly Growing Up.* San Francisco: HarperSanFrancisco, 2003.

Goleman, Daniel. *Destructive Emotions: A Scientific Dialogue with the Dalai Lama.* New York: Bantam Books, 2003.

Goleman, Daniel, Richard Boyatzis, Annie McKee. *Primal Leadership: Realizing the Power of Emotional Intelligence.* Cambridge, MA: Harvard Business School Press, 2002.

Hanh, Thich Nhat. *The Heart of Buddha's Teaching: Transforming Suffering into Peace, Joy, and Liberation.* New York: Broadway Books, 1999.

Kornfield, Jack. *After the Ecstasy, the Laundry: How the Heart Grows Wise on the Spiritual Path.* New York: Bantam Books, 2001.

Ladinsky, Daniel, trans. *The Gift: Poems by Hafiz.* New York: Penguin Books, 1999.

Leigton, Taigen Dan. *Faces of Compassion: Classic Bodhisattva Archetypes and Their Modern Expression.* Somerville, MA: Wisdom Publications, 2003.

Maslow, Abraham. *Toward a Psychology of Being.* Hoboken, NJ: Wiley, 1998.

Peters, Tom, and Robert Waterman. *In Search of Excellence: Lessons from America's Best-Run Companies.* New York: Harper & Row, 1982.

Richmond, Lewis. *Work as a Spiritual Practice: A Practical Buddhist Approach to Inner Growth and Satisfaction on the Job.* New York: Broadway Books, 2000.

Scott, Susan. Fierce *Conversations: Achieving Success at Work & in Life, One Conversation at a Time.* New York: Berkley Books, 2002.

Senge, Peter. *The Fifth Discipline: The Art and Practice of the Learning Organization.* New York: Doubleday Books, 1990.

Sogyal Rinpoche. *The Tibetan Book of Living and Dying.* San Francisco: HarperSanFrancisco, 2002.

Stack, Jack. *The Great Game of Business.* New York: Doubleday, 1992.

Suzuki, Shunryu. *Not Always So: Practicing the True Spirit of Zen.* New York: Harper Collins, 2002.

Suzuki, Shunryu. *Zen Mind, Beginner's Mind: Informal Talks on Zen Meditation and Practice.* New York: Weatherhill, 1970.

Trungpa, Chögyam. *Shambhala: The Sacred Path of the Warrior.* Boston: Shambhala, 1988.

Whyte, David. *House of Belonging: Poems.* Langley, WA: Many Rivers Press, 1996.

ACKNOWLEDGMENTS

In contemplating the hundreds of people who deserve acknowledgment in this book, I can't help but think of an expression from Zen literature: "Awakening is easy; just avoid picking and choosing." Still, there seems to be no avoiding picking and choosing in my wish to thank the people who have deeply contributed to my life and to this book. I offer deep bows to all, knowing my list could be endless and this book is not.

I am especially grateful to Norman Fischer for being my friend, teacher, mentor, and coconspirator in developing Company Time Workshops. We each share a passion for "relieving suffering in the business world" and Norman's vision and generosity touch me deeply. And many thanks to all the participants of these workshops for sharing your stories, your pain, and your dreams — and for teaching me so much about the business world and about myself.

I am grateful to my other core Zen teachers: Suzuki Roshi, whom I never met but with whom I feel a close connection; Richard Baker, Yvonne Rand, Harry Roberts, Mel Weitsman, Lewis Richmond, Michael Wenger, Paul Haller, and Marsha Angus.

The path toward writing this book has been long and winding, as well as short and direct. Bruce Feldman paved the way for me to leave New Jersey and venture to San Francisco, for a one-year leave of absence that turned into ten years. I appreciate every bit of your encouragement. Ed Brown, through writing the Tassajara Bread Book, introduced me to the San Francisco Zen Center.

Much of this book began to germinate during my three-month "sabbatical from my family" when I lived at the San Francisco Zen Center after a twenty-year hiatus as a resident. Having to give talks forced me to think, to write, and to have to say something. Teah Strozer was particularly warm and supportive: "So, what would you like to do? Teach, lecture, spend nights here at the center? You can do whatever you want." Steve Weintraub's support of me cannot be explained, and what words are there to offer thanks?

My apologies for using a sports analogy, and a boxing analogy at that, but, I sometimes feel like a boxer who has had so many people in my corner — a very wide corner — giving encouragement, keeping me in line, keeping the sweat from my eyes, and sometimes fixing cuts: Karin Gjording, Chris Fortin, Meg Alexander, Bruce Fortin, Ed Sattizahn, Linda Ruth Cutts Weintraub, Peter van der Sterre, Steve Stucky, Darlene Cohen, and Carole Harris.

I am grateful to extraordinary business mentors and supporters: Rudy Hurwich, Warren Langley, Shina Richardon, Steve Jacobs, Rob Stein, Rob McKay, Carolyn André, and Gary Sparks.

The Social Venture Network community has been a particular source of friendship and inspiration — Peter Strugatz, Joe Sibilia, Laury Hammel, Deborah Nelson, Pam Chalout, Gretchen Wilson, and many, many other good friends.

I offer thanks to Jennifer Futernick for taking such good care of my mother at Tassajara, for amazing encouragement, and for providing great feedback with this book and ideas to help with the final touches.

My family has watched and supported this writing process, with grace and humor, always raising the bar: Lee, Jason, Carol, Ron, and Ilene.

Working with the New World Library team and my editor, Jason Gardner, has been like a dream. I'll never forget the first time Jason referred to me as one of their "authors." Does the author make the publisher, or does the publisher make the author? Or, does the reader make the publisher and the author? Another Zen/business paradox! Thank you, New World Library, and thank you, readers.

INDEX

H

habitual thinking, 33, 44
happiness, 39–42, 110–11
Hawken, Paul, 175
Heart Sutra, xvi
humor, 29, 211–13

I

impermanence
    energy and, 123
    flexibility and, 143–46,
        207–9
    right concentration and,
        103
    time management and,
        173
information flow, 139
inner voice, 147–50
In Search of Excellence, 238–39
inspiration, 160
integrity, 27
intention, 159–61
    See also thinking
interdependence, 179–81
interrelatedness
    business strategy and, 104
    right livelihood and, 94
    wisdom as experience of,
        131–32
intimacy, 160, 173
inventory projections, 137

investments, 109–10, 184–87
Irish Prayer, 132

J

job changes, 5–6, 237–38
job interviews, 5, 97–98
job rotation, 140
jobs. *See* work
joy, 29

K

killing, refraining from, 114
kindness, 90
koan, work as, 35–37

L

lawyers, 176
layoffs, 89–90, 184–85, 203
leadership skills, 27–28, 86–87,
    230
listening
    deep, 27, 87, 148–49
    radical, 203–5
    skills, 27
livelihood, right, 61, 93–96
lying, 114

M

McMillan, Ian, 199
mail-order businesses, 175

ABOUT THE AUTHOR

Photo by Christopher Sabre

Marc Lesser has been practicing and studying Zen for thirty years and is a Zen priest in the lineage of Suzuki Roshi, author of *Zen Mind, Beginner's Mind*. Marc was a resident of the San Francisco Zen Center for ten years and in 1983 served as director of Tassajara Zen Mountain Center, the first Zen monastery in the West.

He was founder and CEO of Brush Dance, a publishing company that creates greeting cards, journals, and calendars, for fifteen years and currently teaches and lectures in both the Zen and business environments. He holds an M.B.A. from New York University's Graduate School of Business.

Marc is the president of ZBA Associates, a company offering coaching and consulting services in the business and not-for-profit communities. He lives in northern California with his wife and two children. His website is www.zbaassociates.com